The New York Book of Tea

❖ Where to Take Tea ❖
and
Buy Tea & Teaware

Third Edition

The New York Book of Tea

❖ Where to Take Tea ❖
and
Buy Tea & Teaware

Third Edition

Bo Niles

with illustrations by Susan Colgan

UNIVERSE
NEW YORK

First Universe edition published in the United States of America
in 2003 by UNIVERSE PUBLISHING
A Division of Rizzoli International Publications, Inc.
300 Park Avenue South
New York, NY 10010
www.rizzoliusa.com

Previously published by City & Company

2005 2006 2007 / 10 9 8 7 6 5 4 3 2

Third Edition
Printed in the United States
ISBN: 0-7893-0861-4

Library of Congress Catalog Control Number: 2003104745

CONTENTS

A CIVILIZED SIP

Taking tea is a convivial activity, a perfect way for friends—or loved ones, or even business associates—to get together. When this book was conceived, it was planned as a mutual endeavor co-authored with Veronica McNiff, the mother of a school chum of my son's. Together and separately we enjoyed countless cups of tea at the many tearooms, hotels, museums, department stores, and boutiques around town that celebrate tea.

Tea, simply put, is an enigma. What other beverage, after all, makes you feel so utterly of the moment and, at the same time, gently invokes the past and conjures up the future in its leaves? Simultaneously stimulating and soothing, tea rejuvenates and relaxes the body and soul. When you take tea, you replenish your energies and you engage in contemplation. Tea is a tonic.

Loving tea as Veronica and I did—and do—it seemed time, once again, to update this guide, to include new venues that have opened in the five years since our Second Edition. This time, I am flying solo. But, many of the places that Veronica wrote up for the original book (and the Second Edition) remain in this one. For this, I am enormously thankful, so I gratefully dedicate this edition to her.

The most noticeable change in the tea scene is the explosion of Asian teas, notably chai and bubble tea, both milky blends that are flavored or spiced for added zing. In addition to retail shops and mail-order sources, websites abound. A number of these are included in this edition as well.

Many venues used to offer a mere handful of choices of teas; these days some of the most popular venues boast inventories of over a hundred teas—if not more. There is a tea for every taste—and, if you find none that appeal to yours, you can blend your own.

Enjoy!
Bo Niles

The British Tradition of Afternoon Tea

Afternoon Tea, like Christmas trees and Santa Claus, is a tradition that was invented in the Victorian era. Unlike High Tea, which was the meal the British working class returned to after a long day laboring at the factory, Afternoon Tea was a formal, aristocratic affectation that evolved as a genteel ritual punctuating the long interval between lunch and evening supper.

The Afternoon Tea encountered today in New York consists of the traditional three courses, which are usually served simultaneously on a tiered cake stand. The presentation of the entire Afternoon Tea menu allows nibblers to graze at their leisure, but tea takers typically follow the three-course menu. In a formal setup, tea is usually of the loose variety, not bagged. After selecting a tea, the brewing tea and hot water are brought out separately, but in matching pots, perhaps with a tea cozy to keep the tea itself warm. The hot water is replenished at least once during the tea. If you ask for an infusion, you will get herbal tea.

The first course comprises a medley of finger sandwiches made from whole wheat bread, white bread, or a specialty such as pumpernickel bread, cut into bite-sized crustless rounds or rectangles. Traditional fillings include peeled, sliced cucumber; de-stemmed watercress; egg salad; sliced white chicken; and perhaps salmon, shrimp, or rare beef. Some menus try to dazzle you with more inventive fillings, or with relishes to spice up the basics. The second course is usually a scone or two (depending upon whether it is a mega- or a mini-version), accompanied by so-called Devonshire cream—a thick whipped cream—plus a choice of preserves and marmalade. The third course is sweet: petits fours, tartlets filled with lemon curd or berries mixed in custard, miniature éclairs, and a cookie or two.

The traditional three-course Afternoon Tea followed by most of the hotels we went to may be offered at a prix fixe, or à la carte. The à la carte menu tends to be more ample and includes fruit, or a selection of cakes. Some places offer both kinds of service; if so, they typically add a selection of sparkling wines, sherries, and ports to the lineup. Indeed, some hotels like to have you segue into the cocktail hour.

Although teatime, in the British tradition, is a four o'clock rite, most venues in the city have taken liberty with the time frame. Some begin offering tea right after lunch; others, in fact, serve tea virtually all day long. Hotels will take reservations, particularly on weekends and during the holidays. Most of the other venues listed herein are more casual and will simply seat you when you arrive; if you do not want to take a chance, telephone ahead to see if a reservation is necessary.

–Veronica McNiff

Where to Take Tea

Tea is the most welcoming and accommodating of beverages. It can be enjoyed virtually anywhere, be it at home, on the run, or in one of the lovely spots around town dedicated to its service. In New York, the delights of taking tea are as many and varied as are the venues where tea is offered. A formal, traditional Afternoon Tea, with its three-course menu comprising sandwiches, scone, and sweets, can be indulged in with the appropriate fanfare and flourishes at more than a dozen of the city's most prestigious hotels. Because visitors to the city who might request or expect tea tend to gravitate to the grander hotels that cluster in the midtown area, hotel teas reflect this penchant. Tearooms, by contrast, which are genially eccentric by nature, tend to be tucked away in casual, out-of-the-mainstream spots their owners have taken a fancy to. The twin lures of neighborhood and neighborliness are part of their distinctive and cozy appeal. Japanese, Indian, and Korean teas offer a tranquil alternative. For a younger crowd, Chinese bubble teas—sweet and frothy flavored milk tea concoctions accented with plump tapioca "pearls"—and Indian-inspired spiced chai lend a bit of a rush. Finally, a number of department stores, boutiques, and museums do a brisk business in tea, especially in the afternoon when snacking revives flagging energies, and this implies a bracing cuppa, even if it's nuke-brewed with a bag.

Hotel Teas

THE ASTOR COURT AT THE ST. REGIS

2 East 55th St. bet. Madison and Fifth Aves.

❖ 212-753-4500

Hours: Daily 3 P.M. to 5:30 P.M.

Raised on a balustraded dais just inside the front door of the St. Regis, the Astor Court appears to be suspended under a pale, frothy sky, which is encircled by a mythological mural, painted by Zhou Shu Liang, depicting the Greek ideals of peace, harmony, and beauty. In colors of white, gold, and pink, it is as confectionary in spirit as the three-course tea it offers each afternoon. The Court's dozen or so tables cluster around a central statue banked by flowers. Table settings are exquisite: linens from Porthault and porcelain from Limoges, by way of Tiffany ♔ Company, are designs exclusive to the hotel. Tea—black, herbal, or scented (eighteen choices in total)—is presented in silver tea pots to the soothing strains of a harp or a piano. Rock candy sugar sticks, both amber and crystalline, to dip into your tea at whim, add a sweet touch. Champagne, port wines, sherries, eau-de-vie, and dessert wines are also offered for an additional price. If something stronger is desired, proceed into the King Cole Bar, and, while there, take in the famous Maxfield Parrish painting of the slightly dyspeptic king.

Prices: prix fixe, $37.50, with a glass of Champagne, $52.50.

CAFÉ VOGUE AT THE WASHINGTON SQUARE HOTEL

103 Waverly Pl. at the NW corner of Washington Square Park
❖ 212-254-1200
Hours: Monday through Saturday 3 P.M. to 5 P.M.

When our Second Edition went to press, tea at the Washington Square Hotel was served in the CIII restaurant, downstairs and around the corner from the main entrance to the hotel. Since then, the restaurant has changed its name—to the North Square—and Afternoon Tea has relocated to a freshly renovated drinks bar behind the hotel lobby. Every afternoon, except Sunday, a three-course tea can be ordered here before the cocktail hour kicks in. Set discreetly behind a pair of wrought-iron gates, the cafe is a lusciously moody sort of spot that evokes the glamour of a luxury liner, but in miniature. Banquettes lining the walls are clad in matte-black faux pigskin; offsetting these are small, curvy armchairs with copper-toned seats. Tables, octagonal in shape, are copper-colored, too. Floors are set with mosaic, a pattern echoed on the coffered ceiling, which is painted in a cubist manner in subtle earth tones. Walls behind the bar are mirrored; those behind the tables where you take your tea are upholstered in a soft, subtly-patterned mustard-hued velvety fabric. Tea is brought to the table in a pot or a two-cup press; tea sandwiches, biscotti, and scone are presented on a tiered stand. The eight teas, described picturesquely on the menu, are from Serendipitea. Besides the old standbys, these include Burrough's Brew, an organic black tea with a hint of coconut, Chocola Tea, which swirls essences of chocolate and vanilla into black tea and rooibos, and Green Passion & Envy, a blend of Japanese Sencha with passion fruit. And, for those dying for total release from a strenuous day, there's ZZZ, which promotes the calming effects of lavender and chamomile.

Prices: prix fixe three-course Afternoon Tea for one, $10; for two, $18; 2-cup press tea, $3.

THE COCKTAIL TERRACE
AT THE WALDORF-ASTORIA

301 Park Ave. bet. 49th and 50th Sts.

❖ 212-872-1275

Hours: Daily 3 P.M. to 5:30 P.M.

Long a magnet for presidents and proletariat alike, the Waldorf-Astoria sits proudly upon a patch of New York turf just south of St. Bartholomew's Church and a half dozen blocks north of Grand Central Station. Tea service is held in the spacious lounge overlooking the harmonious art deco Wheel of Life at the Park Avenue end of the lobby. Elevated above the lobby's hum of visitors and walk-through pedestrians, the Terrace is a genial oasis in which to enjoy a pot of Darjeeling and a triumvirate of nibbles: scone, mini-sandwiches, and pastries. Islands of cushy seating are well-spaced on the luxurious carpet; huge square columns and a gilt rail further increase the feeling of privacy. At the appropriate time, a piano player situated in the middle of the space signals a segue into the cocktail hour. Four additional tables poised at the corners of the mosaic floor on the lobby level allow people-watchers to sip and speculate at their leisure.

Prices: prix fixe, $32; with a glass of sparkling wine, $42.

FITZERS AT THE FITZPATRICK MANHATTAN HOTEL

687 Lexington Ave. bet. 56th and 57th Sts.
❖ 212-355-0100
Hours: Daily 3 P.M. to 5:30 P.M.

A quiet enclave of Gaelic charm unexpectedly close to the bustle of 57th Street, this is the New York outpost of a family-owned Irish hotel chain. Everyone working here is as Irish and as friendly and disarming as any soul you might care to meet in County Clare. Make a right off the lobby, where the *Irish Echo* and *Irish Voice* lie next to visitors' guides, to find Fitzers Restaurant. Tables are covered with white tablecloths, surrounded by French chairs with a moss-green carpet underfoot. The teatime experience is more like a country hotel tea than a genteel citified four o'clock. The teapot contains two teabags as big as baby pillows; a trio of warm currant scones comes with butter and a huge dollop of strawberry jam. On one visit, two Englishmen nearby tucked into it all—with gusto—while doing business.

Prices: Irish High Tea, $12; Low Tea, $9; pot of tea for one, $3.50; one scone with butter and jam, $2.50.

THE GALLERY AT THE CARLYLE

35 East 76th St. at Madison Ave.

❖ 212-744-1600

Hours: Daily 3 P.M. to 5:30 P.M.

Finding the Gallery is a bit of an adventure as neither of the two entrances into the Carlyle suggest its presence. Your best bet is to access the hotel from its Madison Avenue entrance and proceed up steps, past the Carlyle Cafe and Bemelman's Bar (pause to peek in at the delicious murals by the illustrator of the beloved *Madeline* books). Voilà! The Gallery is really an intimate ante-room to the hotel restaurant. The decor, based on a room in Istanbul's Topkapi Place, is furnished intimately with five tables, a miscellany of kilim-covered sofas of various pedigrees and inclinations, and fringe-trimmed fire-red velvet high-back chairs. The intense mood lighting also adds to the Gallery's mystical ambience. The near-dizzying riot of patterns in the miniscule space is relieved by the jewel-toned palette. One almost expects to be offered a hookah rather than a serious tea, and, as a matter of fact, some of the clientele appear to be anticipating just that. Thick accents and intense hunching over papers is often the modus operandi here. It is as far from the madding crowd as you can get! Next stop: the souk.

Prices: prix fixe, $29; pot of tea, $6; à la carte tea sandwiches, $12; scone or crumpets with clotted cream and jam, $10; and miniature pastries, $15

THE GARDEN CAFE AT THE HOTEL KITANO

40 East 38th St. bet. Park and Madison Aves.

❖ 212-885-7000

Hours: Daily 3 P.M. to 5 P.M.

What a surprise. The Kitano offers not one, but four afternoon tea menus in its spacious Garden Cafe. As you walk through the main lobby, pause to growl back at the Botero sculpture of a dog. The Cafe, a few steps down from the rear of the lobby, is a lofty, naturally lit atrium space with ficus trees. Warm cherrywood panels enclose the walls; the tables and vaguely Biedermeier chairs are solid but graceful; and a large and colorful original tapestry hangs on the west wall. In all, an attractive ambiance that makes you feel cosseted in a world-traveler kind of way. The dainty traditional Afternoon Tea is an excellent standard. But there's also a Japanese Tea Delight and à la carte tea service. Afternoon Spirits adds a choice of liqueurs. Service is gracefully efficient, as befits the value the Japanese set on manners both private and public.

Prices: prix fixe Traditional Afternoon Tea for one, $17.50; for two, $29. Japanese Tea Delight for one, $18; for two, $32. Pot of tea, $3.75. Pastries, $8.50 per selection.

THE GOTHAM LOUNGE AT THE PENINSULA

700 Fifth Ave. at 55th St.; hotel entrance on West 55th St.
❖ 212-247-2200
Hours: Daily 2:30 P.M. to 5 P.M.

Just steps up from the chandelier-lit entrance hall, the Gotham Lounge is a serene oasis, both for hotel guests and for visitors strolling in from shopping or a matinee. Although it overlooks the stair, and is thus somewhat exposed to foot traffic through the lobby and reception area, the buzz of conversation is happily muted by plush carpeting and upholstery and heavy draperies at the windows. A recent renovation left the walls intact; these are painted to simulate a tawny-hued stone, providing the perfect "High Renaissance" backdrop to three framed frescoes depicting arcadian landscapes as well as a series of luminous photographs of books. Furnishings have been updated; gone are the old, velvet club chairs and French-style fauteuils, replaced with a pair of ample sofas between the arched windows looking out to the chocolate walls of the Fifth Avenue Presbyterian Church, and with comfy chairs of various heights and girths that exhibit a subtly Philippe Starckesque swagger. Two tables are inlaid with game boards should you decide to engage in chess or checkers while you sip your tea. The tea selection is concise: five are blended in Hong Kong specifically for the hotel; another seven, including a genial blend called Chameleon, hail from Taylor's of Harrowgate. The four-course Peninsula Afternoon Tea, served on Wedgwood, includes an assortment of tea sandwiches: roast beef with asparagus and brie cheese with truffles and arugula, plus the traditional cucumber, smoked salmon, and egg salad. Scones with Devonshire clotted cream and preserves follow, then a selection of tea breads and pound cake with lemon curd, then fruit tartlets and chocolate pastries. If that isn't enough to satisfy your appetite, the Gotham Lounge is also a bar, so port or sherry, or a flute of Champagne, may be poured to accompany your tea should you decide to extend your repast into the happy hour.

Prices: prix fixe four-course Peninsula Afternoon Tea, $37; with flute of Champagne, $50. Glass of port or sherry, $12 to $25.

ISTANA AT THE NEW YORK PALACE

455 Madison Ave. bet. 50th and 51st Sts.

❖ 212-303-6032

Hours: Daily 3 P.M. to 5:30 P.M.

The courtyard bracketed by the elegant chocolate-colored Villard Mansions—and the tree-accented lobby created to link the two— makes for an imposing entrance into the New York Palace. The hotel, which was originally created by the self-styled Queen of the Palace, Leona Helmsley, occupies a tall glass skyscraper behind the mansions. On the ground level of the hotel, just inside a separate entrance at 51st Street is Istana, the restaurant the hotel uses for breakfast, tea, and drinks. (The hotel is also home to the world-renowned restaurant Le Cirque 2000, which took over the paneled rooms where tea used to be served.) Vaguely Moorish in appearance, Istana is entered through a loggia draped in iridescent silk. High burgundy velvet backs and squooshy, tufted pillows accentuate the comfiness of the banquettes that line the tall, narrow, beam-ceilinged room; tall host chairs, also clad in velvet, pull up to the tables. Chandeliers and sconces play up the glitz. Tea service is the standard three-course affair. The triple-tiered stand, with its galaxy of sandwiches, scone (with clotted cream, but no jam), and miniature pastries is replenished as often as you wish. Teas include an aromatic French Verveine, Earl Grey, chamomile, Darjeeling, and English Breakfast.

Prices: prix fixe three-course Afternoon Tea, $31; with a flute of Champagne, $39.

LADY MENDL'S TEA SALON
AT THE INN AT IRVING PLACE

56 Irving Pl. bet. 15th and 16th Sts.

❖ 212-533-4466

Hours: Wednesday through Sunday 3 P.M. and 4:30 P.M.

This is a really delightful addition to the New York tea scene, named after one of New York's most redoubtable women, the seminal decorator Elsie de Wolfe, who, upon her marriage, became Lady Mendl. Would Elsie approve of this tea salon? Definitely. Eclectic vintage Victorian furnishings and tea things are displayed with artful aplomb. It's all very genteel: conversation is a discreet hum; quiet classical music is in the air. Go light on lunch and prepare yourself for five tea courses. First comes a little taste of fresh seasonal fruits; then a trio of mini-sandwiches; and next a plain or cranberry scone furbished with cream and preserves. This is followed by an offering of sweets and candied citrus peels, and finally, there's an over-generous slice of dacquoise. Choose your tea from a daily selection culled from a stock of thirty, including herbals. Summer brings iced teas, like White Peach. Note: The front stoop is a challenge to climb. But worth it.

Prices: prix fixe, $30.

THE LOBBY AT THE ALGONQUIN

59 West 44th St. bet. Fifth and Sixth Aves.

❖ 212-840-6800

Hours: Daily 11:30 A.M. to 10:45 P.M.

To partake of tea at the Algonquin, or "Gonk," is to sample something of American literary and theatrical history; though alas, the
hotel does not offer a teatime menu as such. Still, it is well worth
a visit for its sense of place. The Algonquin opened its doors in
1902, attracting personalities such as Douglas Fairbanks,
Gertrude Stein, and Eudora Welty. After World War I, Dorothy
Parker, Robert Benchley, and other writers and critics—most of
them associated with the *New Yorker*, just around the corner—
started the Round Table in the hotel's Oak Room, where, over
lunch, they exchanged witty judgment on each other and the cul-
tural events of the day. Recently refurbished, the Algonquin's
lobby has lost none of its charm; its genial melange of squashy
velvet sofas, wingchairs, and armchairs still suggests a clubby
atmosphere of long duration. Reading lights abound, so if you are
in the neighborhood and are so inclined, you can stop in, order a
pot of tea, and while away an hour or so with a newspaper—and
no one will bother you. On our last visit, as we were consulting
the Weekend Section, a jovial group of older gentlemen were
enjoying a round of port while another dozed happily in a corner,
legs stretched out and a muffler pulled up over his nose. During
the Algonquin's renovation, the shabby Rose Room, beloved by
ladies lunching together on their way to a matinee, was incorpo-
rated into the Lobby. This is still the spot to have breakfast or
lunch; the Oak Room opens in time for dinner.

Prices: pot of tea, $4.

THE LOBBY AT THE MICHELANGELO HOTEL

152 West 51st St. bet. Sixth and Seventh Aves.
❖ 212-765-1900
Hours: Daily 11 A.M. to 5:30 P.M.

An aura of hushed formality suffuses the pink marble-floored, two-story high lobby at the Michelangelo Hotel—until 5 P.M. when the drinks crowd descends upon the lounge, which is located in an alcove near the reservations/check-in desk. The rest of the day, though, the lounge is blissfully quiet, so much so that we had to remind the bartender on duty to pull together the tea service that this hotel offers to guests and visitors who happen in off the street. The lounge is comfortably appointed with deep, sink-into sofas, loveseats, banquettes, and armchairs; these coalesce into discrete conversational islands that foster a feeling of privacy and mutual respect. In other words, you can sit virtually anywhere in the lounge and never feel privy to another's tête-à-tête. Colors are low-key: Walls are scumbled a deep mustard hue; upholstery and draperies play off a palette that relies upon muted, earthy shades of green, red-orange, and gold. Lighting, which glows through parchment shades, is subdued and flattering. The Tea Time menu at the Michelangelo is overseen by Limoncello, the restaurant that inhabits the corner of the hotel at the junction of 51st Street and Seventh Avenue. Teas themselves are displayed in chunky glass canisters on a pull-around cart in front of the bar: all are full-leaf; all are fresh and deeply fragrant. A pot of tea is pricey, but the pot itself is robust and pours a minimum of three or four full cups. Tea sandwiches can be prepared on the bread of your choice: white, rye, or whole wheat. A plate of petit fours and miniature pastries is also available. If you are truly hungry, Limoncello also offers a room-service style menu that includes more substantial fare. The drinks menu kicks in at any time.

Prices: pot of tea, $7. Tea sandwiches, $18; petit-four and miniature pastries combination, for one, $11.

THE LOBBY AT THE ROYALTON

44 West 44th St. bet. Fifth and Sixth Aves.

❖ 212-869-4400

Hours: Monday through Friday and Sunday 3 P.M. to 1 A.M.;
         Saturday 3 P.M. to 2 A.M.

The Algonquin and the Royalton face off across 44th Street in one of those New York—style standoffs that makes the city tingle. The Algonquin represents the small, distinguished old hotel tradition; the Royalton is where the new chic crowd of rock stars, top magazine editors, wealthy wannabes, and YBAs (young/beautiful/ambitious of any gender) congregate; the Philippe Starck—designed environment will surely be landmarked around 2050. The gray slate lobby is luxurious in an extraterrestrial, underground sort of way. Starck stretched the long narrow bi-level space even further with a bright blue runway of carpeting which is detailed with Dr. Seuss—like motifs. Tea is served to you as you're seated in oversized Jetson-style seats wrapped in white tie-on napery. While you wait, surreptitiously eye new arrivals as they parade down Starck's catwalk.

Prices: pot of tea, $5; desserts, such as "44" cheesecake, chocolate
          Gianduja cake, or crème brulée, $9.50

THE LOBBY LOUNGE AT THE FOUR SEASONS HOTEL NEW YORK

57 East 57th St. bet. Madison and Park Aves.

❖ 212-758-5700

Hours: Daily 3 P.M. to 5 P.M.

The Four Seasons Hotel, located between Madison and Park Avenues, is one of Manhattan's most recent entries on the hotel scene. The breathtakingly lofty, but austere, lobby of pale stone is visually softened by a carpeted and mirrored balcony where tea is served. The narrow space holds just a handful of tables, sinuous velvet sofas plumped with enormous pillows, and sink-into chairs that encourage lingering. Both black and oolong teas are offered, as well as a trio of aromatic herbals—rose hips, peppermint, and chamomile. The tea menu is sensibly apportioned according to cravings: a traditional three-course Afternoon Tea, with an optional glass of sherry; finger sandwiches, with a tall flute of sparkling wine, if desired; or two freshly baked scone, accompanied, if you wish, by a vintage port.

Prices: prix fixe, $32.

MARK'S AT THE MARK, NEW YORK

25 East 77th St. at Madison Ave.

❖ 212-744-4300

Hours: Daily 2:30 P.M. to 5:30 P.M.

With its matte-polished paneled walls decorated with framed prints of statuary in an array of poses, forest-green carpeting, and velvet-upholstered seating in shades of mustard, rose, and mulberry, the Mark exudes an old-world ambience perfectly suited to its pair of Afternoon Teas: The Mark Tea and The Strawberry Cream Tea. The variables to the two teas are the sweets. The Mark offers petite pastries in lieu of the strawberries and crème chantilly that are the main component of the tea by that name. Both teas feature selection of daily specialty tea sandwiches and pastries. To reinforce the intimate, clubby mood, and to create pools of privacy, Mark's is laid out on three levels, which are punctuated by wrought iron railings, banquettes, columns, and the occasional potted palm. On the lower level, a mammoth floral arrangement girdled with tufted velvet seating takes center stage. Dress code here is casual, running the gamut from stilettos to tennis shoes. Tea may overlap with lunch because Mark's is the hotel's restaurant. The bar swings into action later in the day.

Prices: prix fixe, for The Mark Tea, $23; Strawberry Cream Tea, $21.50.

THE PALM COURT AT THE PLAZA

768 Fifth Ave. bet. 58th and 59th Sts.

❖ 212-759-3000

Hours: Monday through Saturday 3:45 P.M. to 6 P.M.;
Sunday 4 P.M. to 6 P.M.

The Plaza may be the Hollywood vision of what constitutes a grand hotel; it is done with aplomb and the best money can buy. And indeed a fringe of palms define the court, situated in the central lobby. They look as new and flourishing as the rest of the furnishings. There are acres of mirrors, massive marble columns, and plenty of bright gilding lavished on the giant caryatids and the lofty coffered ceiling, with its vast glittering crystal chandeliers. "Better than Fortnums!" exclaimed the Anglophile, lying replete in her comfortable red velvet chair after sampling the prix fixe tea. Service is impeccable; the tablecloth is crumbed between courses; the tea pots are quietly checked for hot water; fresh flowers appear on the table as the blazered musicians launch into Mozart, and then *Les Miserables*. The Palm Court's own tea blend turns out to be Harney's, a Keemun black tea served piping hot and strong. Next: a tray selection of pastries made in the Plaza's own kitchens. A vast silver serving trolley displays all of the possibilities of the house pâtisserie to keep those waiting for a table in delicious torment.

Prices: prix fixe, Traditional Afternoon Tea, $29; High Plaza Tea, $35;
Children's Tea, $19.50. scone, $8; desserts, $9 per selection; glass
of house Champagne, $12.50.

THE ROTUNDA AT THE PIERRE

2 East 61st St. at Fifth Ave.

❖ 212-838-8000

Hours: Daily 3 P.M. to 5:30 P.M.

Enormous murals with a mythological bent encircle this aptly named space furnished with eight tables for tea. Trompe l'oeil society dames strut across a faux-balustraded walk. Satyrs, nymphs, and other assorted types leer and peer from behind monumental columns and revelers and gamblers frolic through a pastorale that seems to mate *A Midsummer Night's Dream* with the oeuvre of some junior apostle in Tiepolo's workshop. The clientele is similarly eclectic: a grandmum, mum, and daughter are prettily poised; a May-December duo are contemplating their next move; beyond, two young things are comparing muscle tone. The traditional tea may be complemented, for a surcharge, with a sparkling wine, port, or sherry. Goodies are also available à la carte.

Prices: prix fixe, $35; Royal Tea with sparkling wine, port, or sherry, $45; Fino Tea paired with sherry, $34; Light Afternoon Tea, $28; à la carte treats, from $15 to $20.

ALICE'S TEA CUP

102 West 73rd St. bet. Columbus and Amsterdam Aves.

❖ 212-799-3006

Hours: Tuesday through Friday 11:30 A.M. to 8 P.M.;
      Saturday 10:30 A.M. to 10 P.M.; Sunday 11 A.M. to 8 P.M.
      Afternoon Tea served "before AND after noon."

On your way to or from Lincoln Center or a West Side movie, or after shopping along Columbus, do stop in at Alice's Tea Cup, named after the plucky heroine who slipped *Through the Looking Glass*. The tearoom—two rooms actually—is a lovely, cozy spot to linger over a cup of tea, and a melt-in-your-mouth, crumble-on-your-bib scone or sweet. Roomy tables provide ample space to companionably spread out and share Alice's cornucopia of freshly baked Afternoon Tea goodies, or happily browse a book or newspaper if sipping solo. Owners—and sisters—Lauren and Haley Fox understand their clientele to—well—a T. They offer not one, but three Afternoon Tea menus, each more ample and scrumptious than the last, as well as a Wee Tea for children under 10, with appropriately scaled yummies. The Nibble consists of a pot of tea (served, intelligently, in a pot with a little sponge slung under the spout to catch drips), a choice of scone with preserves and whipped cream, a choice of sandwich, and a dessert sampling. The Mad Hatter and Jabberwocky up the ante, adding more sandwiches and cookies, and embellishing upon the dessert selection. The most seductive of sweets may be the "White Rabbit Dark Chocolate Mousse with Milk Chocolate Shavings" served in a flowerpot, which is presented, with a flourish, as part of the children's Wee Tea; it can also be enjoyed à la carte by suitably appreciative grown-ups.

Prices: prix fixe Afternoon Teas: The Nibble, $20; The Mad Hatter, $25; The Jabberwocky, $30 (add $20 if sharing); and children's Wee Tea, $12. Three-cup pot of tea, $4; 6-cup pot, $6 (prices slightly higher for rare teas). Chai crème brulee, $8; Queen of Hearts French Verveine tea-infused lemon tart, $6; Jean's Not-Yet-but-Soon-to-be-Famous mocha chocolate chip cake, $6; White Rabbit dark chocolate mousse with milk chocolate shavings, $6.

DANAL

90 East 10th St. bet. Third and Fourth Aves.
❖ 212-982-6930
Hours for Afternoon Tea: Friday and Saturday 4 P.M. to 6 P.M.;
reservations required.

As previously reported, Danal is tucked into a nondescript block on the fringes of the wholesale antiques district. Steps down from the street, the restaurant proper—which is open every day but Monday—is redolent of a summer somewhere in the English shires. The tin-ceilinged restaurant is dominated by a blue tile-covered counter that sets off the kitchen; the dining area is genially furnished with pine tables and mismatched chairs, scrubbed pine dressers, and cupboards filled with crockery and tea pots of fulsome proportions. Tea service, which must be requested in advance, has moved upstairs to the restaurant's recently acquired second-level floor-through. Bright yellow walls, a corner fireplace, oriental rugs scattered higgledy-piggledy over the floor, and a huge front window cheer the room, as do floor-to-ceiling shelves densely packed with dinnerware and glassware of every description. The tea menu is extensive, and embraces many varieties of tea, including one lovely oolong, Goddess of Mercy, which is low in tannin and caffeine. Japanese Sencha is poured warm, not hot, so that it may be properly savored. Several aromatics are also on the list: note Hu-Kwa and smoky Gout Russian Dutchka. Tea accompaniments are something of a surprise, as Danal relies on the chef's fancy when preparing your repast. Danal also caters tea parties for 12 to 50 people. These are especially popular for those celebrating bridal or baby showers.

Prices: prix fixe three-course Afternoon Tea, $20 per person for parties up to ten; for ten or more, $30 per person.

E.A.T.

1064 Madison Ave. bet. 80th and 81st Sts.

❖ 212-772-0022

Hours: Daily 7 A.M. to 10 P.M.

Teatime at this genial Upper East Side to-go/stay-in combo bistro alludes to a special afternoon menu that makes the most of the establishment's fabulous bakery goods, which range from a sumptuous chocolate cupcake to a yummy, overscaled, perfectly proportioned linzer torte or shortbread heart. The tea selection, despite the menu's title, is spartan—just the standard bagged English and Irish Breakfasts, Earl Grey and Darjeeling, plus chamomile. But who cares, when you can indulge your sweet tooth and hang out as you wish? E.A.T., with its mirrored walls and checked floor, bespeaks an industrial efficiency that perfectly suits Madison Avenue mothers. During the interval between naptime and the presupper screamies, little Jennifer and Jason can drool from their strollers—and it can all be wiped up.

Prices: cup of tea, $2; sweets, $2 to $6.

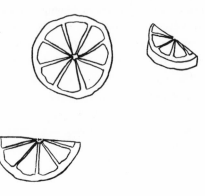

ELI'S VINEGAR FACTORY NEWS CAFÉ

1745 York Ave. at 91st St. or 444 East 91st St.
❖ 212-722-4000
Hours: Daily 7 A.M. to 8 P.M.

Conveniently located across the street from Eli Zabar's Vinegar Factory (see page 100) is the VF News Café. Here the atmosphere is congenial and the clientele mixed—from those taking the air with their dogs and/or strollers along the Carl Schurz Park East River overlook to those who drop in after a workout or swim at the nearby Asphalt Green. The cafe, which can be accessed either from York Avenue or 91st street, offers two styles of taking your tea. During off hours, you may sip and snack at one of the convivial tables or booths in the mellow, wainscoted trattoria section of the cafe; otherwise, hunker down at one of five tiny cafe tables near the newsstand. A full wall is packed with enough periodicals and newspapers to please any journalistic palate—but be warned, whatever you may want to peruse must be purchased before you settle in. Teas, all Twining's basics in bags, are displayed near a thermal carafe of hot water at one end the central island, where breakfast pastries, such as bagels, and the cash register reside. A long counter along the 91st Street wall features baskets of yummy baked goods, all, of course, fresh from Eli's bakery and the VF; one holds brownies and blondies, another, apricot tarts, yet another, mini-palmiers. If you are with a friend, you might like to share a rustic fruit tart. It's just a tad too large to consume solo—unless your workout completely depletes your energies.

Prices: small cup of tea, $1, large cup, $1.75. Brownies, blondies, apricot bars, $2; mini-palmiers, $1.99; pound cake, $2; rustic fruit tart, $2.95. Oversized peanut butter, ginger, oatmeal and chocolate chip cookies, $1.50.

KEKO CAFÉ GOURMET COFFEE
& TEA HOUSE

121 Madison Ave. bet. 30th and 31st Sts.

❖ 212-685-4360

Hours: Monday through Friday 7 A.M. to 8 P.M.;

Tea Time 2:30 P.M. to 6 P.M;.

Saturday 7 A.M. to 6 P.M. (no tea service); closed Sunday

Although it is located across the avenue from the American
Academy of Dramatic Arts, which was designed by renowned
turn-of-the-last-century architect Stanford White, the Keko Café
inhabits an otherwise rather unprepossessing stretch of lower
Madison Avenue. Even upon entry, Keko enchants, its front door
garlanded as it is with ivy and its windows softened with ruffled
lace. Inside, walls covered with architectural engravings, botanical
prints, and urban scenes, and sundry cubbies and shelves packed
to overflowing with teaware, decoupaged boxes, and suitcases all
contribute to an atmosphere of genial intimacy. Leaf teas—21 of
them—are displayed to their advantage behind the pastry counter.
You may choose any one for your in-house pot of tea; you can
also purchase the loose tea to take home, in quantities of 3 oz. or
more. Some of the more exotic varieties to note are an Indian
Spice black tea, a Moroccan Green, and a hibiscus flower herbal
blend. During the workday, Keko obviously services a walk-in
(and take-out delivery) clientele, but during the late afternoon,
tranquility reigns at the café's four petite copper-topped tables.
Tea may be enjoyed in the traditional three-course style, with tea
sandwiches, pastries, and freshly baked scone. If your appetite is
not up the challenge of a full repast, you can order à la carte.
The one discordant note in the whole room is a rather intrusive
TV buckled to the wall in one far corner; thankfully it hangs,
more or less, out of your direct gaze; thankfully, too, it is silent. If
you feel compelled to watch, it is tuned to the Food Channel.

Prices: prix fixe three-course Tea Time Tea, $12.95; small pot of tea,
$3.75, large pot, $4.75.

KING'S CARRIAGE HOUSE

251 East 82nd St. bet. Second and Third Aves.

❖ 212-734-5490

Hours: Daily 3 P.M. to 4 A.M., reservations required

When Elizabeth King met her future husband, Paul Farrell, in his native Ireland, she confessed to him that she'd love to replicate Irish manor-house hospitality in New York. Several years ago, the couple realized that dream, converting a former bookshop in a charming two-story brick carriage house into a place to lunch, dine, and take tea. Their traditional Afternoon Tea is served under the languid gaze of three antlered stags in the sunny yellow Willow Room overlooking a slip of a garden. Here a hot pot of Irish-blend leaf tea is accompanied by comfy cucumber-padded triangles of crustless bread, salmon on toast and curried chicken tartlets, miniature scone with jam, and a tempting array of tiny sweets. Liz and Paul showcase an annual boutique during the Christmas holidays where they sell Irish linens, teas, and assorted treasures collected on trips home to Ireland and England. Tea pots, from J. Sadler, march in a tidy row across an Irish scrubbed pine hutch. The upstairs Red and mural-embellished Hunt Rooms, seating 28 and 16 respectively, are available for private teas; bridal showers are popular.

Prices: prix fixe three-course Afternoon Tea, $16.95; crown-topped and cottage-shaped tea pots, $52.

LE SALON DE THÉ AT LA MAISON DU CHOCOLAT

1018 Madison Ave. bet. 77th and 78th Sts.

❖ 212-744-7117

Hours: Monday through Saturday 10 A.M. to 7 P.M.,

Sunday Noon to 6 P.M.

The Salon de Thé closes one-half hour earlier.

80 Rockefeller Plaza

❖ 212-265-9404

Hours: As above; the bar closes one-half hour earlier.

Even though this is a book devoted to tea, we have been known to sip other potables. Deflated by the mid-morning blahs, for instance, we often grab an espresso con panna. And, then, there's hot chocolate. One recent afternoon, we felt irresistibly drawn to the Upper East Side branch of La Maison du Chocolat. There we discovered, to our delight, the charming chocolate box of a salon de thé, which lies beyond the boutique. Walls covered in fawn-colored faux suede and wall-to-wall carpeting mute conversation at the salon's four petite tables to a genteel whisper. Teas include a tawny Darjeeling and a Ceylon, as well as Melange La Maison du Chocolate, a sultry Chinese blend perfumed with the "natural aromas of seven citrus fruits." The raison d'etre of the salon de thé, of course, is the seductive menu of sweet treats. Flavored mousse cakes—Negresco, Andalousie, and Bresilien, among others—feel as luxuriant upon the tongue as their mellifluous names. Equally generous are their macaroons, which are plump, pillowy, and offered in two styles: chocolate filled with chocolate ganache and coffee/almond filled with mocha ganache. Then, there's the Degustation Platter: seven select pieces of chocolate. Superbe! At both locations, there's also a bar for those desirous of a quick pick-me-up—be it tea, coffee, or hot chocolate. You can also purchase chocolate milk in bottles to take home or to your desk.

Prices: two-cup jug of tea, $4.50; Guayaquil or Caracas hot chocolate, $7.
Mousse cakes, $6, Bacchus truffle mousse infused with raisins flambéed in rum, $6, 4/4 Citron gateau, $3.50; Pleyel chocolate almond cake, $4.25; Macaroons, $4.25. Degustation Platter, $8.

LE SALON DE THÉ AT FAUCHON

442 Park Ave. at 56th St. ❖ 212-308-5919

Hours: Monday through Saturday Noon to 6 P.M.

FAUCHON

1000 Madison Ave. bet. 77th and 78th Sts. ❖ 212-570-2211

Hours: Monday through Friday 7:30 A.M. to 7 P.M.;

Saturday 9 A.M. to 7 P.M.; Sunday 10 A.M. to 6 P.M.;

tea is self-service all day long.

From Park Avenue, one can peep through Fauchon's plate glass
window into its genteel Salon de Thé, which is screened from the
bustling shop it inhabits by a curved partition—Fauchon's wall of
teas. Within, all is calm and luxe. The dozen tables are set with
crisp white cloths and Fauchon's signature rosy-rimmed porcelain.
Because of its reputation for fabulous patisseries, Fauchon is not a
place to be discreet, especially when the waiter proffers their
menu for Afternoon Tea. First your tea: Fauchon sells about 100
different teas, in every variety from black to green to white—take
your pick, then stir it, if you desire, with a crystallized sugar stick.
The first course of the Afternoon Tea consists of a plate of
canapés and mini-sandwiches; goose fois gras from Perigord is
one filling you will find nowhere else. The desserts that follow
include petits fours, teacakes, pillowy moelleux made with almond
paste, macarons, and chocolates. You may also order tea à la
carte, and here, one sublime indulgence stands out: the Megeve,
layers of vanilla meringue, chocolate mousse, and chocolate
ganache that has been in Fauchon's repertoire for 80 years.
Quelle merveille! Uptown, at the Madison Avenue shop, tea is a
simpler affair. Order a pot and select a sweet from the patisserie
case, then perch at a cafe table at the back, where teas, spices,
condiments—and Fauchon's cookbook—are displayed.

Prices: Le Salon de Thé prix fixe two-course Afternoon Tea, $30; pot of
tea, $8; select rare teas, $12; cup of Matcha tea, $5. Plate of tea
sandwiches, $15; plate of teacakes, $10. Tarts, $8. Plain croissant,
$4; brioche, or pain au chocolat, $4.50.

Prices: Fauchon on Madison cup of tea, $2.50; pastries vary according
to selection.

LEAF STORM TEA

Corner of 94th St. and Amsterdam Ave.
❖ 212-222-3300
Hours: Monday through Friday 7:30 A.M. to 5 P.M.;
Saturday 8:30 A.M. to 5 P.M.; closed Sunday.

Like Seinfeld's infamous Soup Nazi, one-time clothing designer
Amy Chen—a much more welcoming proprietor, to be sure—oper-
ates her take-out "spot of tea," Leaf Storm, out of a mere sliver of
a space, a bump-out really, barnacled to the side of an Upper
West Side apartment building just off Amsterdam Avenue. Here,
she has set up a jewel box of a tea emporium, which showcases
32 teas in gleaming, silvery canisters set into cubbies along the
wall behind the serving counter. The tea selection visibly attests to
Amy's months-long immersion in the art of creating, brewing, and
drinking tea. Leaf Storm, therefore, not only carries familiar varieties of teas and herbals, such as English Breakfast, Lapsang
Souchong, chamomile, and rosehips, but it also dispenses a honey-
like organic rooibos, a spicy chai, and three exquisite oolongs,
including Goddess of Mercy—which might be just the ticket after a
hard day at the office. Leaf Storm teas are brewed from loose
leaves, which are measured into silky, oblong pouches; the pouches are generously scaled to allow the leaves to dance in the water
as they steep. Toothsome go-withs include miniature cupcakes lavishly slathered with icing. In warm months, Amy sets out a couple
of tables on the sidewalk for those who are in no hurry to leave.

Prices: cup of tea, $1.60. Miniature cupcake, $2. Sampler kit of 10 teas,
$12.50, of 15, $35.

MICHANNA FINE TEA & COFFEE

109 St. Mark's Pl. bet. First Ave. and Ave. A

❖ 212-979-1650

Hours: Monday through Thursday 11 A.M. to 10 P.M.;
Friday and Saturday 10 A.M. to 11 P.M.;
Sunday 10 A.M. to 8 P.M.

Open just over a year, Michanna is snugly situated just a few steps west of Tompkins Square. Even though the diminutive space can only accommodate five tables (plus a couple of sidewalk tables in warm weather), it boasts an inventory of over 100 teas, which are handsomely displayed in large tins along one wall. Each row of tins is cast in a different pale metallic hue, each shade signifying a particular type of tea, be it black, green, decaffeinated, or herbal. The teas are sold in 2-, 4-, 6-, and 8-oz. quantities; if you like, you may ask owners Don and Won to custom-blend two or three for your take-away packet or mini-tin. Other brands of teas sold here are Grace's Rare Teas, Taylor's of Harrowgate, Yorkshire Gold, Rishi, and Harneys. There's also an organic green-tea concentrate you may add to the beverage of your choice. The blackboard hanging next to the serving counter lists Michanna's menu of ready-to-pour teas, which may be sipped on site or brewed to go. Especially popular are Don and Won's healing teas sweetened with honey: ginger, citrus, date, ginseng, and Chinese quince. Michanna also sells a small but discriminating array of tea things, both Western and Eastern in influence. Chubby Chatsford-style pots come with lids in contrasting hues; some sit in their own cup—or on a warmer. Earl's Court drip catchers are available here, as are infusers, plus a variety of honeys. Michanna will also make up gift baskets upon request.

Prices (include taxes): small cup of "healing" tea, $2.77; large cup (or iced), $3.23. Tea-to-go, 12-oz. $1.70, 18-oz. $1.80, 20-oz. $2.30. Chai tea latte, $3 or $3.50. Pick-your-own-tea honey tea latte, $3.50 or $4. Slice of cake, $1.55; brownie, $2; crispy rice square, $2.50. Tea sachets for the bath, $1.75 each, $3 for two.

PAYARD PATISSERIE & BISTRO

1032 Lexington Ave. bet. 73rd and 74th Sts.

❖ 212-717-5252

Hours: Daily 7 A.M. to 11 P.M.; tea service 3 P.M. to 5 P.M.

Payard, named for award-winning pastry chef François Payard, emerged like a phoenix from a graffiti-scarred storefront on an antiques-and-bookstore swath of Lexington Avenue. Here Payard has created what must be every Francophile's fantasy of the Parisian patisserie. Just inside the front door you'll find pastry cases filled with every sinful indulgence you ever dreamt of—from tiny truffles to extravagances such as the dozen fanciful confections named for some of the most famous monuments and chateaux in France. Payard is tidily divided into three comfortable, chocolate-and-buttercream-hued spaces: the entry shelters a lively coffee-liquor bar, which leads into a sumptuous banquette-lined dining area uplifted with a mezzanine. We sank into our three-course "Thé" in one of the corner banquettes. Nearby, well-behaved children sipped Payard's delectably rich hot chocolate. Payard's special tea is a lemon/bergamot-infused blend.

Prices: prix fixe three-course Le Thé, $19; Le Tea Royal, with caviar and
blini $24; pot of tea, $5. Sweets and confections priced variously.

SARABETH'S

1295 Madison Ave. bet. 92nd and 93rd Sts.

❖ 212-410-7335

423 Amsterdam Ave. bet. 80th and 81st Sts

❖ 212-496-6920

Hours: Monday through Friday 8 A.M. to 4 P.M., then 5:30 to 11 P.M.;
Saturday and Sunday 10 A.M. to 10 P.M.

New Yorkers are divided as to which Sarabeth's they prefer—
though it is not a matter of taste, per se, since the same Sarabeth
comfort foods such as lemon cake, pumpkin muffins, oatmeal,
milk-and-cookie plates, and preserves (which grown-ups just eat by
the fruity, palate-piquant spoonful) are available at either location.
If you head for the Sarabeth's on Madison, you will notice it is a
little more dressed up to suit this cachet neighborhood, with its
boutiques and Corner Bookstore (one of the last bastions of
adventurous literacy in the city). The Madison Avenue Sarabeth's
is full of tapestry-clad banquettes, flowers in baskets, brass chandeliers, and a vast two-story paned glass window that makes you feel
as if you are inside a giant dollhouse. The West Side Sarabeth's is
more informal, with white-painted wainscotted walls. Order from
the desserts/teatime menu.

Prices: prix fixe Afternoon tea, with finger sandwiches, $12.50; with sand-
wiches, scone, cookies, jam, and "clabber," $18.50; pot of tea, $2;
cake with whipped cream and strawberry, $6; muffin with dollop of
jam, $2; milk and cookie plate, $6.

T SALON & T EMPORIUM

11 East 20th St. bet. Broadway and Fifth Ave.

❖ 212-358-0506

Hours: Monday through Saturday 9 A.M. to 8 P.M.;

Sunday 11 A.M. to 8 P.M.;

Proper Afternoon Tea is served all day long.

The ground-floor T Salon, painted a brilliant mandarin orange-red, is where—all day long—you may partake of a full-scale, proper tea, which includes three types of sandwiches, a wedge of Earl Grey chocolate cake, tea cookies, fresh fruit, and nuts. Upstairs, in the T Emporium, the look is fairly madcap—a mélange of attic and general store. Here, proprietor Miriam Novalle showcases her large, eclectic collection of tea things; these commingle with (mainly) late nineteenth-century wares she is happy to part with, for a price. Shelved here, too, is an enormous assembly of giant canisters bearing labels Miriam designed in a collage-y style to evoke an atmosphere of wanderlust—or a cabinet of curiosities. Teas number in the hundreds—300, to be exact, including those she customizes for restaurants and others who seek her counsel. These days, one of her preferences is white tea, subtly blended with "fragrances" of mandarin, jasmine, and rose. Two other favorites: Tibetan Tiger, with "notes" of caramel, chocolate, butterscotch, and vanilla; and Healing Heaven, a first-aid kit in a cup, which blends jasmine and lotus flowers with echinacea, St. John's Wort, cats claw, and lemongrass. Tea accoutrements abound, from standard strainers and infusers to Agatha's Bester Reusable Filter to the Reon Tullensieb, a metal catch-all bristle that slides into the spout of a teapot to entrap stray leaves. The front section of the emporium boasts a huge wooden table; this space is often reserved for private parties.

Prices: prix fixe Proper Afternoon Tea, $32; small pot of tea, $4; large pot, $5. Wedge of Earl Grey chocolate cake, $8; 20-layer crepe cake, $12; scone with clotted cream and jam, $5.

TEA & SYMPATHY

108 Greenwich Ave. bet. Seventh and Eighth Aves.

❖ 212-807-8329

Hours: Monday through Friday 11:30 A.M. to 10 P.M.;
Saturday and Sunday 10 A.M. to 10 P.M.; tea service,
Monday through Friday 11:30 A.M. to 6 P.M.;
Saturday and Sunday 1 P.M. to 6 P.M.

If your average lovable British mum opened a tearoom, this might be it. Ten tables with strawberry-printed oil cloths are squeezed into this tiny space; there are pictures of royalty, and an impromptu collection of bulldog pictures pasted right onto the painted walls. The menu speaks from the heart with British fare such as baked beans on toast, scotch eggs, and hot Bovril. There is Sunday dinner (lunch to you) with roast beef and Yorkshire pud, at least until the food runs out, the waitress disarmingly confides. In summer, there is iced tea. Ask them to add Ribena, a black currant syrup much in favor over there. They even sell Tizer, a fizzy orange drink popular in the 1950s. When English patrons slide in for their cuppa, they request toast with Marmite, held to be a sure cure for homesickness. Ordering the cream tea, a West Country specialty, means scone with real clotted cream: thick, sticky, and delicious. If your cravings linger, stop in at Carry On, Tea & Sympathy's tea–and trifles (touristy and otherwise)– emporium next door.

Prices: prix fixe Afternoon Tea, $18.95; scone, cream, and jam, $4.95;
Cream Tea, $7.95; pot of tea, $3.

TEANY

90 Rivington St. bet. Orchard and Ludlow Sts.

❖ 212-475-9190

Hours: Daily 9 A.M. to 1 A.M.; Monday through Friday Afternoon Tea
Special 2 P.M. to 8 P.M.

Although Teany bills itself as a vegetarian restaurant, tea's the
thing here. From a Matcha-tinged wall to its extensive list of teas—
94 and counting—tiny Teany (only a dozen metal tables pack tight
in the room, and a couple more on the teenier terrace out front)
proclaims its preference for this salubrious brew. Indeed, the fat
little metal notebook set on your table tells you as much as you
need to know about tea: production methods of the various types
from black to green to white; caffeine counts; even health benefits.
A few choice teas that caught our eye were #24 Monkey Picked
Superior Ti Kuan Yin, an oolong with an "orchid-like" flavor
whose leaves and buds are, indeed, plucked by simian fingers;
#87 Tea for the Liver, for those suffering the after effects of a
looooong night on the town; #86 Tea for Flu, and #23 Green
Tea Anemone, whose leaves are hand-tied in the shape of a
flower. Teas are stored in chunky white canisters behind the
cook/serve area. Tea sandwiches include ploughman's cheddar
and pickle, veggie ham and cheese, cucumber and butter, and avo-
cado and cream cheese. Scone varieties also number four: plain,
raisin, blueberry, and cranberry. A pair of sandwiches and a scone
can be enjoyed as part of Teany's Afternoon Tea Special, along
with a pot of Earl Grey Crème, English Breakfast, or Herbal
Vanilla Berry Cream tea. Not to say the tea choice might change:
Owners Moby and Kelly constantly experiment with the menu.
When we stopped in, sake teas were next on the tasting agenda.

Prices: prix fixe Afternoon Tea Special, $10, with a slice of vegan cake,
$12; pot of tea, from $3.50 to $8.50, depending upon selection;
plate of tea sandwiches, two for $6, four for $10; scone, $2.50,
with clotted cream and jam, $4.

VERITHÉ

❖ 212-366-4623

www.verithe.com

For those who want their tearoom to come to them, there's Verithé, "an international tea salon" founded by creative-media consultant-cum-caterer Debbie Samuelson. Launched in 2001, Verithé produces tea "experiences" for groups as intimate as two or as large as 50. Her first big break actually involved an even larger party: a French-style Breakfast Tea for Revlon, who entertained 72 beauty editors over the course of two days. Besides her French Tea, Debbie also produces a Japanese Bente Box Green Tea, and a Moroccan Tea; sample menus can be reviewed on her website. As we go to press, Debbie is researching Chinese tea and Indian tea with the hopes of adding them to her roster—but such teas can be requested even now, as a "customized tea experience." Verithé's additional customized pleasures include personalized tea tastings as well as specialized services, such as a green-tea pedicure.

Prices: The prices for tea experiences vary depending upon the number of guests and the menu. Verithé's website also offers handmade tea candy lollipops on organic rosemary sticks; a small package of six costs $15; a large one, which also includes six, is $20.

YAFFA'S TEA ROOM

353 Greenwich St. or 19 Harrison St.

❖ 212-966-0577

Hours for Afternoon Tea: Daily 2 P.M. to 6 P.M.;
reservations required at least 24 hours in advance.

Yaffa's Tea Room has its own entrance on Harrison Street, or it
can be entered through the zebra-painted door to Yaffa's original
venture, a quirky neighborhood bistro bar on the corner of
Greenwich Street. If, like many others, you have ventured downtown to visit Ground Zero or St. Paul's Chapel, a stop-off at
Yaffa's might be just the respite you need. Yaffa is rightfully proud
of her tearoom's wainscotted interior with its tin ceiling; she spent
months combing flea markets for the eclectic furnishings and finds
that compose the fanciful décor. The High Tea menu includes
petites croques monsieurs or ´dames, croutons with gravlax and
dill sauce, and petits choux with mushroom duxelle or egg salad.
Warm scone with marmalade or jelly and butter follow, then a
selection of Yaffa's home-baked desserts. Slivers of pear tarte
tatin, chocolate truffle cake, or tiramisu, for example are presented together like flower petals on a plate. There are 20 loose teas
that can be brewed to your request, ranging from lemon and jasmine herbals to that old stalwart Earl Grey. Because of Yaffa's
Moroccan heritage, a peppermint tea is also on the menu.

Prices: prix fixe weekday three-course Afternoon Tea, $20; Weekend
Afternoon Tea, $25; glass of port or Champagne, $6 and up.
Small pot of tea, $2.50; large pot, $3.50. Pear tart, carrot cake,
key lime pie, $5; cheesecake or chocolate truffle cake, $6.

Department Store Teas

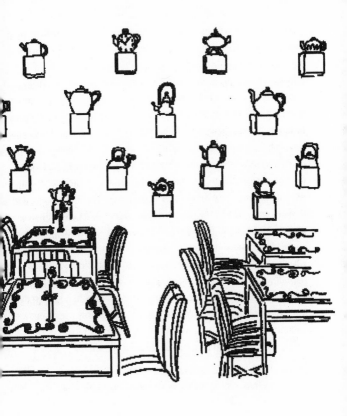

BLANCHE'S AT DKNY

655 Madison Ave. bet. 60th and 61st Sts.
❖ 212-222-3569
Hours: Daily 11 A.M. to 7 P.M.

As any fashionista worth her Daily Candy knows, Madison Avenue bristles with boutiques that appear to be as much about architecture as adornment. Many shops, like the art galleries they emulate, follow a more-or-less minimalist aesthetic. Clothes and accessories are presented with the same finesse as fine art, and, if some of the clothes look better on the hanger than on the all-too-un-minimalist human form, so what? Leaving fashion aside for a moment, though, shopping often stirs cravings more animal than sartorial. Recognizing this, DKNY at 60th Street tucked a chic counter—Blanche's—in one corner of the second level of its spacious two-story shop. Anyone can stop in at any time for a bite—or cup of tea. These come from +AZO and Yogi Tea; most are herbals and decaffeinated blends, although +AZO's Awake can be poured for those in dire need of a jolt. Besides salads and sandwiches, Blanche's also serves cookies of stupendous girth and a variety of amply endowed muffins. Hardly the diet for size 2s and 4s, but you may find you need to pump up your carbs when you size up the bar stools that look as if they'd been hand-hewn by a disciple of Paul Bunyon. While you sip, check out the monitors behind the counter; these replay the latest from DKNY's runways, which may inspire another riffle through the racks.

Prices: mug of tea, $2; hot chai tea latte, $4; fresh-brewed iced tea, $3.
          Muffins, cookies, brownies, and blondies, $2.50. NB: Cash only, no
          credit cards.

BODUM CAFÉ ☙ HOMESTORE

413-415 West 14th St. bet. 9th and 10th Aves.

❖ 212-367-9125

Hours: Monday through Saturday 10 A.M. to 7 P.M.;
       Sunday Noon to 6 P.M.

Founded in Copenhagen in 1944 and now headquartered in
Switzerland, Bodum—named after its founder Peter Bodum—has
long been equated with well-designed, eminently practical teakettles and coffeemakers. Last year, the company made the jump
across the pond to open its flagship store on American soil.
Located just west of the gritty convergence of the avenues defining
the meatpacking district, Chelsea, and the West Village, the airy,
white-walls-and-blond-wood, Scandinavian-style Homestore was
designed, as are all Bodum products, by an in-house team led by
master designer Carsten Jorgensen. A prominent feature of the
cavernous, 6,500-square foot space is a 30-foot-long tea-tasting
bar (where you can also have a snack). The bar is located within
easy reach of the store's wide selection of tea pots and presses,
kettles, mugs—and Bodum's justly famous Tea Wall. Here, under a
photographic frieze illustrating the easy 1-2-3s of how to "press"
the perfect cup of tea, Bodum displays 100 name-brand blends,
which include some basic blacks and greens, as well as myriad
rooiboses and herbal infusions. Each tea is accompanied by a
"tasting" canister—much like the counters dispensing perfumes in
your favorite department store; if you want to taste a few blends
before committing to a final purchase, Bodum invites you to ask
the waiter behind the bar to brew your samples, for $1.75 per
sample cup. Depending upon the time of day, you may want to
take your tea with a light lunch, or with a pastry. All edibles are
displayed in cases at the street-end of the bar. Before you leave,
don't forget to pick up Bodum's recipe for Teapuccino, Bodum's
version of chai.

Prices: cup of tea, $1.75. Scone, cookie, or brownie, $2.

CAFÉ ON 5IVE and
GOODMANS AT BERGDORF GOODMAN

745 Fifth Ave. bet 58th and 69th Sts.

❖ 212-753-7300

Hours for Afternoon Tea: Monday through Friday
2:30 P.M. to 6 PM.

Bergdorf Goodman now hosts not one but two soignée places to enjoy lunch—or tea: the redecorated Café on 5ive, and Goodmans, a brand new venue located down a short flight of stairs in one corner of the store's recently opened, lower-level Beauty Floor. Upstairs, the hive that is 5ive is abuzz with the hum of contented conversation. Travertine marble floors are the color of nougat; lighting is indirect and utterly flattering. Cushy black leather banquettes and ash-blond chairs designed by Arne Jacobsen draw up to tables handsomely draped in white cloth, then topped with crisp-cut squares of paper. The waitstaff, like all of Bergdorf's personnel, seems to exemplify what the last word in poise and fashionable self-awareness ought to be. The clientele, smartly turned out in ultra chic outfits, look equally as cool. Downstairs, at Goodmans, the mood is rather more serene. Painted a whisper-soft celadon and featuring an enormous pixel-like mural that depicts a luxuriant, if ghostly, buffet, the room is anchored by a long central table, plus two rows of intimate seating—on one side, at round tables, along the other at square ones. No need for fancy napery here; the tables are topped with ivory-toned plastic laminate; napkins are a like hue. Sleek cylindrical glasses filled with fresh roses strike the only note of color; otherwise, the focus is on the food, and, as upstairs, on conversation. Both venues offer ten different teas from Harney & Sons as well as a galaxy of sweets.

Prices: Café on 5ive prix fixe two-course Afternoon Tea, $9.95; pot of tea, $2.25. Apple pound cake, warm apple tart or brownie with ice cream, carrot cake, or cookie plate, $4.95.

Prices: Goodmans pot of tea, $2.75. Plate of tea sandwiches, $11; lemon tart, $5.50, carrot cake, $5; cookie plate, $5.50.

CAFÉ SFA AT SAKS FIFTH AVENUE

611 Fifth Ave. bet. 49th and 50th Sts.

❖ 212-753-4000

Hours for Afternoon Tea: Monday through Friday
3 P.M. to 5 P.M., with live harp music

Far be it for you to collapse halfway through your shopping day from sheer hunger, so Saks created its eighth-floor cafe for judicious breaks for elevenses, lunch, and tea. The cafe has recently been redecorated in a more subdued vein. Walls are now striated a warm, tawny shade of cognac and trim is a deep, honey-hued maple; floors are carpeted with crumb-hiding tweed. Because the cafe tends to be less crowded at teatime, you should find yourself happily ensconced at one of the cozy tables in the perimeter loggia. On the 50th Street side, tables take in the twin spires of St. Patrick's Cathedral. On the Fifth Avenue side, you find yourself hovering over an intimate, secret lawn atop one of Rockefeller Center's lower-scaled buildings. From this vantage point, you may also snatch a glimpse of an agile skater performing a double axel on the Rock Plaza ice rink. As you begin to unwind, your repast arrives on a tiered stand bearing cobalt blue plates arrayed with assorted tea sandwiches, crumbly homemade scone and muffins accompanied by Devonshire cream and jams, gourmet cookies, and chocolates. Teas, provided by San Francisco-based Mighty Leaf Tea, come in ten flavors, including the aptly named Celebration, a China black infused with the scent of Guyan fruit, which almost brought us to our feet. On every table there is a chubby and mesmerizing snow-globe: Ours drizzled flakes upon an ur-Manhattan scene clustering St. Pats and Saks cheek-by-jowl with the Empire State Building, Brooklyn Bridge and lovely Lady Liberty herself.

Prices: prix fixe three-course Afternoon Tea, with chocolates, $18.50, pot
of tea, $3.75. Plate with two scones, butter and jam, $3.50.
Cookie plate, $5.75. Saks' signature cheesecake, $5.95.

CREED ON BOND

9 Bond St. bet. Broadway and Lafayette St.

❖ 212-228-1732

Hours: Monday through Saturday 11 A.M. to 8 P.M.; Sunday Noon to 6 P.M.

CREED ON MADISON

897 Madison Ave. bet. 72nd and 73rd Sts.

❖ 212-794-4480

Hours: Monday through Saturday 10 A.M. to 7 P.M.;
Sunday Noon to 6 P.M.

Since 1760, the Parisian firm of Creed Perfumer has been the purveyor of fine scents, by appointment, to European royals such as Kings George III and IV and Queen Victoria of England, Queen Dona-Maria Christina of Spain, and France's Empress Eugenie Napoleon III. In Manhattan, Creed offers its elegant and refined "vintage and ready-to-wear" perfumes—as well as teas—to New Yorkers at two venues, one in Soho, the other on the Upper East Side. The loft like space downtown also hosts an equally elegant salon de thé in a library-like, wood-paneled area at the back of the shop where teas, all from Harney & Sons, are sold. Here, three plush wingchairs upholstered in brilliant Indian fabrics gather around a huge Moroccan brass tray set atop a stand on an Aubusson-style rug. A desk and desk chair occupy one corner of the room if you have a sudden urge to pen a *billet doux*. The entire mise-en-scène glows in the sunlight that streams into the room through a south-facing wall of leaded glass. Creed on Bond graciously pours their (gratis) tea of the day—one afternoon last fall the flavor was mango fruit—into a white porcelain cup, and leaves you to contemplate which of their dozens of teas and perfumes you might wish to swoon with at home. Signature teas for purchase at both locations are Creed's 2000 Flowers and, logically enough, Creed's Bond Street and Creed's Madison Avenue Blends. These are available in 4-oz. tins. Harney's Palm Court Blend for the Plaza Hotel can be purchased here as well.

Prices: cup of tea, at Bond Street location only, free.

THE MAD TEA CUP AT BURBERRY'S

9 East 57th St. bet. Madison and Fifth Aves.

❖ 212-371-5010 or 212-407-7100

Hours: Monday through Saturday 10 A.M. to 6 P.M.;
      Sunday Noon to 6 P.M.

Manhattan, it seems, is mad for plaid, especially of the ubiquitous Burberry variety. Although street vendors peddle knock-offs galore, the real thing is most copiously displayed at Burberry's recently renovated emporium on East 57th Street. Here, too, you can also nibble on plaid cookies baked in the shapes of Burberry's classic wares, including trench coats, umbrellas, and Wellingtons. These goodies—and tea—are found at The Mad Tea Cup on the shop's third floor, where civility reigns at an 18-foot-long communal table surrounded by sleek white-leather-clad barstools that would be the envy of the Mad Hatter himself. And no wonder; Burberry's invited the owners of Alice's Tea Cup, a fairy-tale shop and tearoom on the Upper West Side (see page 23), to oversee their tea venue. Open all day long, The Mad Tea Cup offers ten varieties of tea, all of which were blended especially for the shop. Burberry Blend, for instance, is a Lapsang Souchong—based tea lightly sweetened with butterscotch, while Trafalgar Square infuses an African black tea with mint. The Covent Gardens Blend combines the essences of hibiscus, rosebuds, and rosehips. Teas are presented in pots accented with Alice's idiosyncratic—and utterly practical—tea-drip catchers, to ensure nothing spills on your Burberry's (or other) purchases. The Mad Tea Cup also sells drip catchers along with a selection of lovely, fat tea pots, infusers, and strainers, and teas in 2-, 4-, and 6-oz. packages. Other goodies include chocolate bars, each of which is wrapped with a love letter or love sonnet enclosed. More tea pots can be found on Burberry's Home Floor just upstairs; note the Mad Tea Pot with its top hat, and another that sports a trench coat and muffler—Burberry's, of course.

Prices: prix fixe three-course Mad Hatter Tea, (two tea sandwiches, two scones, and selection of desserts), $35; 3-cup pot of tea, $6. Two scones with preserves, $7; with tea, $10. Burberry's trench-coated people cookies, $12 apiece. Drip catchers, $10.

NICOLE'S AT NICOLE FARHI

10 East 60th St. bet. Fifth and Madison Aves.

❖ 212-223-2288

Hours for Afternoon Tea: Monday through Saturday

      3 P.M. to 5 P.M.;

      Sunday, brunch only, Noon to 4 P.M.

Steps off Fifth Avenue, in the heart of the chicest shopping in town, is the Nicole Farhi boutique. A svelte, soaring space accessed by a gangplank, the shop was designed by Michael Gabellino not only to showcase Farhi's line of clothing and accessories, but also, on its lower level (as at its New Bond Street, London, address), to highlight Farhi's affinity for fine food. A wide, open-tread walnut stairway zigzags down to a landing graced by a handcrafted settee from the Nakashima studio, and thence, past the glassed-in kitchen overlook where Nicole's chefs ply their trade, into the discreetly lit restaurant. At the front of the room stretches a long translucent bar that's lit from within, emitting a seductive glow. In the hours between luncheon and dinner, Nicole's serves food at the bar, as well as a restorative afternoon tea in the dining room proper. The à la carte tea menu features ice cream and sorbet as well as an assortment of cookies. The cookie selection changes from time to time; when we last checked in, chocolate peanut butter, oatmeal cherry, golden raisin cornmeal biscotti, and coconut lemon "thumbprint" were on the menu. Teas, nine of them, are from Fortnum and Mason. Homemade lemonade and fresh-squeezed orange or grapefruit juice are also available, as is hot chocolate.

Prices: pot of tea, $3. Assorted cookies, ice cream, or sorbet, $4.

Museum & Gallery Teas

AQ CAFÉ AT SCANDINAVIA HOUSE

58 Park Ave. bet. 37th and 38th Sts.

❖ 212-847-9745

Hours: Monday through Saturday 10 A.M. to 5 P.M.;
Tea for $2, 3 P.M. to 5 P.M.; closed Sunday

Designed by architect James Polshek of Polshek Partnership
Architects, Scandinavia House occupies a double-townhouse-wide
sliver of Park Avenue in Murray Hill. The mission of the center is
to "showcase the culture of the five Nordic nations—Denmark,
Finland, Iceland, Norway and Sweden"—and that includes
Scandinavia's food, which can be enjoyed in the center's airy
ground-floor AQ Café. The cafe, corralled by pale lattice like fenc-
ing and ficus trees and furnished with plainspoken tables encircled
by Arne Jacobsen's classic Ant chairs in primary hues, is just
inside the front door, and is open to the public even when the galleries upstairs are not. Operated by Aquavit and overseen by that
restaurant's executive chef Marcus Samuelsson, the AQ Café
offers classic Scandinavian dishes, such as gravlax and Swedish
meatballs. More to the point for this guide, though, it also caters
to those in need of a quick afternoon pick-me-up by offering Tea
for $2, which is served between 3 and 5 p.m. Tea for $2 consists
of a bracing mug of one of Harney ℭ Sons bagged teas (you
make your choice from an open tea box on the counter) and a
baked goodie from a daily selection. For a mere $2 extra, you
might try AQ's signature Sweedie, a soft-as-a-cloud, meringue-
topped wafer shaped like a gnome's hat, which is slathered in
hard white chocolate, or dark chocolate, or dark chocolate dipped
in coconut. Yum!

Prices: Tea for $2, includes mug of tea and an oversized cookie or other
selected sweet; mug of tea, $1.25; fresh-brewed iced tea, $1.25.
Oversized cookie, $1.50; brownie, $2.10; Sweedie, $2.

CAFÉ SABARSKY AT THE NEUE GALLERIE NEW YORK

1048 Fifth Ave. at 86th St.

❖ 212-288-0665

Hours: Saturday, Sunday, and Monday 11 A.M. to 6 P.M.;
the cafe is also open on Wednesday and Thursday when the
museum is closed; Friday 11 A.M. to 9 P.M.; Closed Tuesday

Rarely does a new museum open in New York, so it was no surprise when lines formed around the block to visit the Neue Gallerie, the mansion-museum dedicated to early twentieth-century German and Austrian art and design. Conceived—and bankrolled—by the U.S.A's former ambassador to Austria, collector/philanthropist Ronald S. Lauder, the Neue Gallerie, once the home of Mrs. Cornelius Vanderbilt III, has been impeccably restored. Not the least of the museum's pleasures is the Café Sabarsky (named for co-founder and art dealer Serge Sabarsky, a friend of Lauder's who died in 1995), an elegant, wood-paneled recreation of a turn-of-the-century Viennese café. Lines form here, too, and no wonder: Rich and evocative details abound. Banquettes in the high, sunny Fifth Avenue windows are upholstered in rose-dappled velveteen in a 1912 pattern by Otto Wagner; cafe tables are encircled by bentwood chairs after an 1899 design by Adolf Loos; lighting fixtures are a period Josef Hoffman design. An enormous, seasonal floral arrangement dominates one end of the room. Although the cafe is open all day, it is particularly appealing at teatime, when a pot of Ceylon or chamomile-lavender or pineapple-papaya tea (or a caffe mit schlag) perfectly offsets a patisserie created by chef Kurt Gutenbrunner. Do try the Mandel Meringue, the strudel, or—so temptingly Viennese—the Linzertorte.

Prices: pot of tea (served on a little tray with a glass of water alongside),
$5; pastries, $4.50 to $6.

CAFÉ WEISSMAN AT THE JEWISH MUSEUM

1109 Fifth Ave. at 92nd St.

❖ 212-423-3317

Hours: Monday, Tuesday, Wednesday 11 A.M. to 5:30 P.M.;
        Thursday 11 A.M. to 7:30 P.M.;
        Friday 11 A.M. to 2:30 P.M.;
        Sunday 10 A.M. to 5:30 P.M.;
        Closed Saturdays, as well as major Jewish holidays

The handsome and comfortably appointed Café Weissman is located on the lower level of the mansion that once belonged to Felix and Frieda Warburg, which has been the home of the Jewish Museum since 1947. In 1993, the landmark mansion, designed in 1908 as a late French Gothic style chateau by C. P. H. Gilbert, underwent a meticulous expansion and restoration under the direction of architect Kevin Roche, who masterminded various expansions to the Met. Miraculously, the Jewish Museum decided to transform a dated 1960s addition into a replica of the chateau. In Roche's seamless renovation, you cannot tell where the old building leaves off and the new one begins. Although the Café Weissman is a full-service facility offering a pleasant array of soups, salads, and sandwiches, it is also a wonderful spot to meet a friend and enjoy a quiet cup of tea and a pastry, especially if you are zigzagging from one museum to another along Museum Mile. Teas are offered by the bag only, in a tea box on a counter along the wall; you make your selection—all Celestial Seasonings, except for the ubiquitous Brisk Lipton—and steep it yourself in hot water provided in the appropriate thermal carafe. Sweets include individual-portion pecan and apple pies, lemon tart, and chubby wedges of marble cheesecake and chocolate cream pie.

Prices: cup of tea, $1.50; pastries, $4.25.

GARDEN COURT CAFÉ AT ASIA SOCIETY AND MUSEUM

725 Park Ave. at. 70th St.

❖ 212-570-5202

Hours: Tuesday through Thursday, Saturday and Sunday
11 A.M. to 4:30 P.M.; Friday 11 A.M. to 9 P.M.; Closed Monday

One of the true oases in the city is the Garden Court Café—and, one might add, the Asia Society itself. A soothing atmosphere pervades the entire building. Taking tea here—or a meal—is truly a sensuous experience. "Dedicated to fostering understanding of Asia and communication between Americans and the peoples of Asia and the Pacific," Asia Society was founded in 1956 by John D. Rockefeller III. It moved into its present building, designed by Edward Larrabee Barnes, in 1981. A couple of years ago, an extensive overhaul of the building was masterminded by architect Bartholomew Voorsanger. One noteworthy feature of the renovation is the bright blue laminated glass stair leading to the galleries. The café is a dramatic, yet tranquil, glass-enclosed space that seems to lean into 70th Street. Tables share the airy, skylit room with five delicate, weeping podocarpus trees and evocative sculptures by Asian artists, including three "angels" hovering in pods in a work entitled *Flying in a Coccoon* by Indonesian sculptor Heri Dono. Afternoon tea consists of a selection of sandwiches and pastries, plus Asian teas and tisanes—there are 16 to chose from—which are available at other times of the day as well. One delicious cooler is a fruit blend iced tea called Lili´uokalam. The AsiaStore on the other side of the lobby presents an extensive range of Asian tea pots, including Chinese Yixing clay tea pots and Japanese cast-iron pots with warming stands. Wooden tea ceremony boxes, bamboo scoops and whisks, and boxed loose-leaf teas by Serendipitea round out the gift shop's selection.

Prices: kettle of tea, $4.50; plate of assorted cookies, $7; double-chocolate truffle cake, crème anglaise and green tea ice cream, $8.50.

THE MUSEUM CAFÉ AT THE GUGGENHEIM

1071 Fifth Ave. bet. 88th and 89th Sts.

❖ 212-427-5682

Hours: Sunday through Wednesday 9 A.M. to 6 P.M.; Thursday 9 A.M. t
3 P.M.; Friday and Saturday 9 A.M. to 8 P.M.; Closed Monday

Tucked under Frank Lloyd Wright's cantilevered coil, the Museum
Café can be accessed both from Fifth Avenue at 88th Street, and
from the museum proper. The cafe's twenty black granite-topped
tables sit upon industrial gray carpeting. A series of portholes set
into the exterior wall allows pinhole peeping from the sidewalk.
To inspire small talk, the exterior wall and the wall at the back of
the cafe are blanketed from the chair rail to the ceiling with oak-
framed photographs documenting the museum and luminaries
associated with its history, including Wright himself in his signature hat and cape. Bagged tea is served in glass mugs throughout
the day, along with a selection of fresh-baked goodies, including
muffins and brownies that can be picked up, cafeteria-style, from
sleek-brushed steel counter running virtually the entire length of
the room. A special treat is the moist and chewy lemon curd cake

Prices: mug of tea, $1.25.

SARABETH'S AT THE WHITNEY MUSEUM OF AMERICAN ART

945 Madison Ave. bet. 75th and 76th Sts.

❖ 212-570-3670

Hours: Tuesday Noon to 3:30 P.M.;
Wednesday through Friday 11:30 A.M. to 4:30 P.M.; Saturday and Sunday, brunch menu, 10 A.M. to 4:30 P.M.; Closed Monday

At the base of Marcel Breuer's upended brutalist ziggurat and behind a two-story facade of glass is Sarabeth's, a full-service eatery where bagged tea is always at the boil, and a dessert menu is primed to sweeten the palate. The two dozen white-clothed tables, modernistic tapestry-clad and vaguely ergonomic chairs and robust ironstone are positioned upon the slate floor with enough space between them to ensure a restful ambience for catching up on buzzwords and bon mots as well as on the elusive pleasures of the Biennales, both here and abroad. On the way out, stop off and refresh yourself with the ingenuous ingenuity of Calder's Circus at the top of the stairs.

Prices: cup of tea, $1.75; dessert, $6.

Asian Teas & Teaware

FELICITEA

167 West 83rd St. bet. Columbus and Amsterdam Aves.

❖ 212-712-1500

Hours: Winter hours 11 A.M. to 8 P.M.;

Summer hours 9 A.M. to 11 P.M.

Bubble teas are all the rage downtown (and in some outposts in Brooklyn), but none were available north of the Great Divide— 14th Street—until recently. Mel Caylo, one of the five co-owners of FeliciTea—set out to rectify this omission by taking over the front room of a subterranean flower shop called the Enchanted Garden on the Upper West Side. The bubble tea bar is a sunny little room painted a buttery shade of yellow, and it holds only four tables, one of which is wrapped by a welcoming banquette. On each table stands a glass container enclosing a cheerful Kelly-green divot of new grass, a Central Park Great Lawn in minia-ture. During the warm months Mel sets up more tables on the sidewalk and in Enchanted Garden's pocket-sized garden out back. The tea menu focuses on two types of tea, frothy milk teas in a half dozen flavors, and bubble teas, which are similar in taste but include the requisite tapioca pearls that must be slurped up through a fat neon-orange straw. Either version can be enjoyed hot or cold. Straight-forward cups of Chinese black, jasmine green, and Chrysanthemum tea are also available. Because FeliciTea primarily caters to a take-out trade (Crunch, a popular gym, is right across the street), tea is served in a to-go paper cup. Mel plans to bring in china mugs and dinnerware when he adds food to the menu.

Prices: hot or cold cup of milk tea, $3; hot or cold bubble tea with tapioca pearls, $3.50; Chinese black tea, jasmine green tea, $2; Chrysanthemum tea, $2.50. Buy ten bubble teas and FeliciTea will give you one free.

GREEN TEA CAFÉ

45 Mott St. bet. Bayard and Pell Sts.

❖ 212-693-2888

Hours: Sunday through Thursday 10 A.M. to Midnight;
Friday and Saturday 10 A.M. to 2 A.M.

Bubble-tea bars literally "bubble" along the heavily trafficked stretch of Mott Street between Canal Street and the courthouses just north of City Hall. With its brick walls, Asian-style tables and stools, and a sociable, young-in-spirit clientele, the Green Tea Café is one of the cheeriest along the route. The café serves a dozen versions of bubble and frothy milk teas plus a number of greens, blacks, and fruit/flower combos. Flavorings for the bubble and milk teas range over the gustatory map, from taro to wheat germ to mint to ginger. Besides tea, the café also rustles up milkshakes spiked with green or red bean, chocolate, honeydew, coconut cream, or strawberry, and a series of specials that includes a bubble coffee as well as a sweet concoction blending coffee, tea, and honey. Tasty accompaniments include sandwiches, snacks, dumplings, or toast, the last slathered with cream of coconut or peanut, or condensed milk—or, for those loathe to give up their English Afternoon Tea, strawberry jam. This being Chinatown, you can also order a variety of cold noodle dishes, Szechuan spicy eggplant, and other Chinese specialties.

Prices: hot or cold bubble tea, $3.75; hot or cold milk tea, $3.50; green tea, $3.75, black tea, $3.50. Pot of flower/fruits tea, from $6.50 to $7.25. Flavored milkshake, $3.75. Bubble coffee, 75¢; Toast, $1.85; dumpling with black tea, $3.75.

ITO EN

822 Madison Ave. bet. 68th and 69th Sts.

❖ 212-988-7111

Hours: Monday through Saturday 11 A.M. to 7 P.M.,
   Closed Sunday

Anyone who recalls that old Upper East Side fixture on the
restaurant scene, the Right Bank, will be mesmerized by the
serene new Japanese tea boutique that occupies that space: Ito
En. Ito En (and Kai, its companion tearoom upstairs, see page
61) describes itself as dedicated to "creating new traditions in the
art of tea." Designed by Yohi Shiraishi of Yoshi Design NY, with
counters and tables handcrafted from cherry wood by Jeffrey
Brosk, and flower arrangements by Eve Suter, the space where
teas and tea things are displayed exudes an atmosphere of healthful calm. Ito En treats their teas with rigorous respect: All, except
samples showcased in tall, elegant sake bottles on shelves inside
the front door, are stored in two large, humidity-controlled refrig-
erators kept at a constant 40 degrees. This precaution is taken to
insure that the fragile leaves retain their flavor, without drying out.
Tea is measured out into "nitrogen-flushed" nylon sachets (which
brew two cups); these are vacuum-sealed in small foil packets
holding five sachets apiece. Descriptions of Ito En's 75 teas are
as poetic as their styles. Some varieties to explore are roasted
teas, bright teas, and rice tea. Ito En carries a selection of arti-
sanal tea wares, including Bizen-yaki, one-of-a-kind pieces fired in
the Bizen kiln, the "oldest of Japan's six great kilns." Accoutrements
used in the tea ceremony, including matcha bowls, tea caddies,
bamboo whisks, vases, and trays, are also available. Ito En's gift
boxes are especially handsome: They look like hatboxes, but are
made of stained and lacquered wood. A miniature travel set
includes a matcha bowl, mini-whisk, and tea caddy. Books include
Okakura's classic *The Book of Tea* and the gloriously illustrated
Book of Tea published by Flammarion. Ito En also sells bottled
iced teas in three flavors.

JADE GARDEN ARTS & CRAFTS COMPANY

76 Mulberry St. at Canal St.

❖ 212-587-5685

Hours: Daily 10 A.M. to 7 P.M.

Jade Garden sells a plethora of latter-day Chinese arts and crafts, but the real reason to visit this shop is its selection of Yixing teaware. The ageless refined forms suggest the calm serenity of the infinite. Collectable Yixing "violet sand" earthenware tea pots are shaped from rarely occurring, naturally colored clay deposits in a rural region of northern China. The small pots are traditionally used for Yunnan teas, which are brewed very strong and served in tiny tea bowls. The potters of Yixing province still create refined, matte-glazed tea pots in shapes that have not changed for centuries. The "violet sand" fires to a variety of muted colors: violet-toned terracotta, taupes and leafbrowns, a green-tea hued olive tone, and various subtle blues in cerulean and indigo tints.

KAI

822 Madison Ave. bet. 68th and 69th Sts.

❖ 212-988-7277

Hours for Afternoon Tea: Tuesday through Saturday
2:30 P.M. to 4:15 P.M. (please call ahead);
Closed Sunday and Monday

Sharing the harmony and hospitality of the Japanese tea culture—and the experience of Japan's hallowed tea ceremony, but without the esoteric formalities—is the avowed aim of Kai, the restaurant that recently opened on Madison Avenue on the site formerly occupied by the Right Bank. On the ground level is Ito En, a purveyor of teas and tea things (see page 59); Kai is upstairs. Kai is discreetly compartmentalized into two areas, a narrow sushi bar at the back, behind a gauzy curtain, and the more commodious—yet still intimate—restaurant, which is open for luncheon and dinner as well as afternoon tea. Upholstered banquettes the shade of silver-tipped tea leaves and black tables and chairs set off the color and texture of the food. Kai means gathering place; the word is also short for *kaiseki*, the delicate little nibbles that enhance the tea ceremony. Kai's Full Afternoon Tea consists of two trays of nibbles, one savory and one sweet, and a pot of tea. Savories, prepared by executive chef Hitoshi Kagawa and executive sous chef Daisuke Horai, include a selection of diminutive tea sandwiches, tea-flavored onigiri rice balls, a tiny quiche, and two mini-scones, one flavored with green tea. The sweets tray features wasabi cookies, a Lilliputian slab of chocolate cake, matcha-covered almonds, grapefruit peels dusted with powdered Earl Grey tea, and a miniature crème brulee that is also flavored with a hint of tea. Tea flavors are exotic and wonderful: these include Chinese chrysanthemum, Jasmine Pearl, Megami Sencha—toasty Hoija, and stone-ground Matcha—and, for those of a traditional British-style bent, Wild Mint, chamomile, and Earl Grey. Kai also has a pair of private rooms downstairs, either or both of which can be reserved for a tea tasting or other event. These are reached by a path of stepping stones that appear as if glazed by rain. They are meant to slow down your passage and lead you to into a contemplative frame of mind.

Prices: prix fixe Full Afternoon Tea, $24; pot of tea, $6 to $8, depending upon the rarity of the tea. Sweet Tray, $12; Savory Tray, $10. Kai's unsweetened, bottled iced Tea's Tea, $3.50.

61

KELLEY AND PING

127 Greene St. bet. Prince and Houston Sts.
❖ 212-228-1212
Hours: Daily 11:30 A.M. to 11 P.M.

The front of this self-styled Asian grocery and noodle shop at the Houston Street end of boutique-lined Greene Street is devoted to tea—to both its sale and sipping. One entire wall is lined with shelves holding enormous canisters that dispense two dozen teas, whose very names might inspire poetic indulgences: Iron Goddess of Mercy, Gen Mai Cha, Gunpowder, and Chrysanthemum are just a sampling. Teas in tins—Spice, Lotus, Lemon, and Vanilla—and accoutrements, such as clay tea pots and bowls, are displayed upon a shelf just behind the two tables and toadstool perches where tea can be taken—along with mooncakes from Taiwan, egg custard tarts, or coconut tarts, and assorted small cookies.

Prices: pot of tea, $2; mooncake, $1.75.

KINOKUNIYA BOOKSTORE

10 West 49th St. at Rockefeller Plaza

❖ 212-765-7766

Hours: Daily 11 A.M. to 7 P.M.;

Wagashi served Fridays from Noon to 7 P.M.

Wagashi are traditional Japanese confectionaries that originated in sixteenth-century Kyoto and evolved into an art form meant to engage all five senses. Some forms of *wagashi* are created as an elegant testament to the seasons; others are made and served to honor special occasions. In Manhattan, the Toraya shop and tea room (see page 72) is the principal purveyor of these delicacies, but on Friday afternoons and evenings you can also sample them at the tiny bar toward the back of the Japanese Kinokuniya Bookstore, which lies directly across from the ice-skating rink on the south side of Rockefeller Plaza. The rest of the week the tea bar offers a selection of more Manhattan-minded sweets, including chocolate soufflé cake and chestnut cream cake—plus green tea tiramisu. Kinokuniya highlights a number of books about tea and the Japanese Tea Ceremony in the English-language section of the shop; in this section they also carry an extensive range of Japanese literature translated into English, as well as books on architecture, design, gardening, crafts, and health.

Prices: cup of tea, $3.25; cup of Matcha tea, $3.25; cup of Gokura tea, $5.41; iced Matcha, $3.79. Wagashi, $4.33 per piece.

PEARL RIVER MART

477 Broadway bet. Broome and Grand Sts.
❖ 212-431-4770
Hours: Daily 10 A.M. to 7:20 P.M.

Pearl River bills itself as a Mart, and so it is—20,000 square feet
of wall-to-wall merchandise spread throughout two levels, on and
below the street. The company's business card also proclaims that
"we bring interesting things to New York," and it does this, too.
Many of the wares Pearl River carries echo those you'll find in
Chinatown, but there is more here—including lots and lots of fun
and funky items, as well as bin after bin of practical little necessi-
ties, which make trolling Pearl River a real treat. Prices are so
low and the inventory so seductive, you cannot leave without purchasing something. In terms of tea and tea things, Pearl River carries dozens of styles of tea pots, tea cups, handle-less tea bowls,
and all manner of infusers, strainers and the like. Sections devoted to tea are on both levels of the Mart, so it pays to make a full
circuit of the store before finalizing your decision about what you
might like to take home. Besides teaware, Pearl River sells a wide
assortment of teas, both full-leaf and packaged. Tins of tea come
from a number of manufacturers such as Foo Joy, whose offerings
include Lungching Premium Green, Jasmine Silver Pearls,
Imperial Keemun, and a tea poetically called Before the Rain.
Another brand, Mr. Chan, offers a Jasmine in a tin printed with
pictures of simpering ladies. One entire section of the Mart is
devoted to Dieter's Teas. In addition to these, Pearl River carries
a selection of 80 full-leaf varieties. These are displayed in large
glass containers along the wall in the mini tea bar, which occupies
a balcony at the back of the main floor. These teas can be purchased by the ounce; you can also request a pot of tea and sip it
on site at one of the balcony tables. If you can't make up your
mind, eight teas are displayed in little dishes set on a tray on the
tea counter; these are meant to inspire your choice.

Prices: pot of "regular" tea, $3.50; pot of premium tea, $5.50.

SAINT'S ALP TEAHOUSE

39 Third Ave. bet. 9th and 10th Sts.

❖ 212-598-1890

20 Elizabeth Street, bet. Canal and Bayard Sts.

❖ 212-227-2880

Hours: Monday through Thursday 1 P.M. to Midnight;
       Friday and Saturday 1 P.M. to 1 A.M.;
       Sunday 1 P.M. to 11 P.M.

Oriented toward the student crowd at nearby New York
University, Saint's Alp Third Avenue Teahouse is defined by an
off-beat, fast-food ambience of faux wood wainscoting and bright
backlit photos of tasties to go. Saint's Alp, a "premier purveyor of
Taiwanese tea," is justifiably proud of its Frothy Tea with Pearl
Tapioca, aka bubble tea, replete with chewy pearls rolled from a
blend of sweet potato, cassava root, and brown sugar. Saint's
Alp's bubble tea flavors include coconut, peanut, almond, taro,
sesame, and wheat germ; some are made with black tea and some
with green. All flavors can be purchased hot or cold in two sizes,
the 14-oz. regular or 20-oz. jumbo. Saint's Alp also offers a wide
selection black and green teas, as well as fruit-flavored milk teas,
and chai.

Prices: Frothy-tea with pearl tapioca, $2.85–$3.85; green tea,
       $2.45–$3.35; milk tea, $2.45–$3.45. Toast, $1.50.

SARA INC.

952 Lexington Ave. bet. 69th and 70th Sts.

❖ 212-772-3243

Hours: Monday through Friday 11 A.M. to 7 P.M.;
       Saturday Noon to 6 P.M.

Though it specializes in modern Japanese ceramics, Sara's contemplative aesthetic springs directly from Japan's ancient tradition of studied-but-spontaneous beauty in form and technique. (The name Sara is actually the Japanese term for dish.) In the window, glass, ceramic, and wood objects for partaking of tea or dining form a tranquil still-life composition. Inside the white shell of the store, table furnishings that range from brilliant-hued and playful to pure and ascetic repose on massive built in ledges. Owner Kumi Oniki directly imports ceramics from Japan, and most are exclusive to the store in this city. Two free-standing oak tables present table settings that combine Japanese forms with Western culinary requirements. Elegant *furoshiki*—patterned cloths used in Japan for wrapping and carrying things—serve as napkins, placemats, or very special giftwrapping. Tea things abound for both Japanese and Western style service. While we visited, an American potter came in to talk over some of the new pieces with the manager. But if you glaze over at discussions of ceramic technique, submit instead to captivation at their effects.

TAKASHIMAYA NEW YORK and
THE TEA BOX AT TAKASHIMAYA

693 Fifth Ave. bet. 54th and 55th Sts.

❖ 212-350-0100

Hours: Monday through Saturday 10 A.M. to 6 P.M., except Thursdays
10 A.M. to 8 P.M.; The Tea Box Tea hours: 3 P.M. to 5 P.M.
Closed Sunday

Takashimaya is a sublime six-story repository of ultra-refined fash-
ions for the home and person, with a cross-cultural sensibility that
embraces the best of Tokyo, Paris, and New York. Tea things are
displayed with the Home Collection on the third floor, as well as
in the anteroom to The Tea Box on the lower level. The selection
of Japanese tea pots and bowls is complemented by lacquerware,
linens, and meticulously stitched leatherbound blank books and
boxes. The few conspicuous British-style tea things seem incongru-
ous, but it must be nice for some to know they are there, just in
case they have a yen for something in which to serve Earl Grey. A
highlight of the lower level is a footed tray, or tea box, which contains the elements—such as a miniature bamboo whisk needed to
whip up a froth on green tea—that are essential to Chado, the tea
ceremony. Smartly tailored, paper-sheathed boxes behind the
counter hoard loose teas that can be purchased by the ounce.

Each of the Tea Box's two tearooms are a study in the interplay
of gentle geometries and the soft neutral tones of sand and stone.
The rear room, a sanctuary of calm, is ringed with banquettes
banked with soft, linen-clad pillows, and lit by tiny mesh-encased
halogen bulbs. A luncheon menu segues seamlessly into the
Afternoon Tea, which features The Tea Set, a pot of tea (there
are 37 to choose from), accompanied by a trio of exquisite cookies, either butter-based by West and Yoku Moku, or Vegetable by
Suetomi. An East-West Afternoon Tea includes fresh fruit and
Bernachon chocolates flown in from Lyons. An à la carte menu is
also available.

Prices: prix fixe for The Tea Set, $6.50; East-West Afternoon Tea, $14.50.

TAMARIND TEAROOM

41-43 East 22nd St. bet. Madison and Park Aves.
❖ 212-674-7400
Hours: Monday through Friday 10:30 A.M. to 10 P.M.

Located right next door to the serenely beautiful Indian restaurant of the same name, Tamarind's hankie-sized tearoom holds a mere five tables and a narrow counter for two. Teas here—14 in all—are displayed in big square glass jars on shelves behind a backlit service bar, which also showcases a variety of sweets. Sets of vivid, psychedelic renderings of the gods Shiva and Natraj supply the only other decoration in the room. The mood here, then, is like a refreshing cup of tea—soothing, yet snappy. True to its indigenous cuisine Tamarind offers a menu of delicious Indian sweets and sandwiches (as well as some Brit-style pastries), pairing each dish with the appropriate, recommended tea. Thus, for example, you might want to taste Nan Khatai spiced lentil flour shortbread with a cup of organic Darjeeling, or a pair of nut-and-semolina-filled pastry twists called Bon Bons with a Ceylon orange pekoe. Spicy Masala Chai is generally taken with cake rusks, Indian biscuits you are meant to dunk in your tea. Of the sandwiches, Saag Paneer incorporates a filling made from garlic-accented spiced spinach and homemade cheese; it is meant to be accompanied by a subtle oolong called Ti Kuan Yin (or Tieguanyin), while the pickled tandoori mushroom-filled sandwich called Achari Khumb takes a Japanese green Genmaicha perked up with roasted, popped kernels of rice. A robust, malty black Assam goes with the Lamb Sholley, whose lamb filling marinated in yogurt and spices is drizzled with a minty yogurt dressing. Tamarind also offers two multi-course teas, for one person or for two; these include a pot of tea, a choice of one or two sandwiches (from the listed six), and a platter of assorted pastries. When you order tea à la carte, there's a minimum cover of $7.50.

Prices: prix fixe two-course tea for one: $15; for two, $25; pot of tea, 75c.
Indian specialties: Nan Khatai, $2.50; cake rusks, $1; Bon Bons,
$4.25. Indian sandwiches: Saag Paneer or Achari Khumb,
$6.25; Lamb Sholley, $7.95. Fruit tart, $4; scone or muffin,
$3; pound cake, $4.95.

TEA & TEA

51 Mott St. bet. Bayard and Pell Sts.

❖ 212-766-9889

157 Second Ave. bet. 9th and 10th Sts.

❖ 212-614-0138

1588 Broadway at Times Square

❖ 212-586-9368

58-01 8th Ave., Brooklyn

❖ 718-437-6622

Hours: Daily 11 A.M. to 11:30 P.M.

Tea & Teas are unpretentious, faux-rustic, student-oriented fast-food hangouts which, in addition to a line-up of fried and steamed Asian delicacies, serve up over 30 green, black, and frothy milk teas and bubble teas, as well as a tasty selection of milk shakes, barley teas, and smoothies (including a green-tea one). Tea & Tea prides itself on its exotic drinks; several of these—Passionate Temptation, Verdant Cooler, and Crimson Sensation—are refreshed with green tea. As in many a Chinese restaurant, you make your Tea & Tea selection by number: the aforementioned Passionate Temptation, for example, is #67, while a simple black tea with nothing in it checks in at #19. Teas can be ordered hot or cold, in the regular 14-oz. size or large 20-oz. size. House specials and 'recommendations' such as hot Ginger Black Tea and Ice Roasted Oolong are bulleted.

Prices: hot or cold Frothy Milk Tea with Pearl Tapioca, regular, $2.85 to $2.95; large, $3.75 to $3.85. Hot or cold plain or flavored green and black tea, regular, $2.45; large, $3.35. Green Tea Smoothie, $2.95. Toast, $1.50. Japanese Mushi Soft Cheesecake, $2.35. Two jumbo tea eggs, $1.70.

TEN REN TEA AND GINSENG COMPANY

75 Mott St. bet. Canal and Bayard Sts.

❖ 212-349-2286 and 212-349-1937

Hours: Daily 10 A.M. to 8 P.M.

Mail-order: 800-292-2049

www.tenrenusa.com

This glittering, streamlined emporium is a branch of a Taiwan-based corporation, where many of the teas served and sold are grown; other teas are from China. Of Ten Ren's multiple outlets in the U.S., New York has three, one in Manhattan, one in Flushing (at 135-18 Roosevelt Ave.; 718-461-9305), and one in Brooklyn (5817 8th Ave.; 718-853-0660). As you walk into the Mott Street shop, owners Ellen and/or Mark Lii will pour you a tiny cup of golden-hued green tea, which you can sip as you scan the meticulously organized interior. A wide range of black, oolong, and green teas are sold here, all stored and displayed in large gold-metallic canisters along the wall behind the counter. Two of Ten Ren's finest teas are Tung Ting Oolong and Pouchong Green Tea; there are six grades of each from which to select. If you are uncertain about which teas you may wish to purchase, there is a tea-tasting table at the rear, where calligraphy and a wall painting set the mood—as does a collection of contemporary teaware, some of which are also offered for sale. For those who cannot get to Chinatown, Ten Ren prints a glossy mail-order catalog, which illustrates which teas are sold loose as opposed to those packaged, in tea bags and tins. Ten Ren also offers American-grown ginseng, both wild and cultivated, in tea or in capsules—and a ginseng candy. A 'family package' of green tea powder (7.5 oz.) is accompanied by a flyer extolling the health benefits of green tea.

TEN REN'S TEA TIME

79 Mott St. bet. Canal and Bayard Sts.
❖ 212-732-7178
Hours: Daily 10 A.M. to 9 P.M.

Two doors down from Ten Ren Tea and Ginseng Co. is the parent company's latest offshoot, a snappy bubble-tea bar where you can sample the traditional teas for which Ten Ren is justifiably renowned, as well as some of the trendiest tapioca teas in town. The three dozen teas are offered hot or iced, with or without fruit infusions, in "regular" or "double" portions. Tapioca pearls also enhance fruit, nut, bean, and green-tea flavored shredded ices, and iced milk shakes, one of which blends coffee and tea for a particularly sweet buzz. Ten Ren's tea treats don't stop there: Along with your beverage, try a tea snack or tea dessert, as many of the youthful downtown twenty-somethings do who hang out at the tables at the back of the shop. Green tea is a major ingredient of a number of edibles, including tea eggs, green-tea noodles, and green-tea scone, so, if you are on jury duty, say, and need a quick fix, just stop in, grab a fat neon-colored straw, and take away a tapioca tea. Just try not to slurp until a verdict is reached.

Prices: Tapioca Traditional Ice Tea, 12-oz. 'regular' size, $3.50 to $4; 24-oz. 'double' size, $4.50 to $6; Tapioca Fruit Iced Tea; 12-oz., $3; 24-oz, $4.50; 12-oz. Tapioca Hot Tea, $3 to $4. Ten Ren Traditional Tea, 12-oz. size, $3 to $4. Green tea scone, $1.50. Tea jellies, $1.50. Tea egg, 75¢.

TORAYA

17 East 71st St. bet. Fifth and Madison Aves.
❖ 212-861-1700
Hours: Monday through Friday 11 A.M. to 6 P.M.;
        Saturday 11 A.M. to 7 P.M.;
        Closed Sunday

Occupying the ground floor of a townhouse off Madison Avenue, Toraya is a magnet for visiting Japanese who want to partake of their native *wagashi*, a confection the Japanese consider an enticement for all five senses and the perfect companion to their delicate, native green tea. Toraya's tea shop, devoted to the presentation and sale of boxed confections, is as tidily designed as a tea chest, containing oak cabinetry so finely crafted that the joinery appears virtually seamless. The tearoom itself, located in the back, feels like an architectural rendition of a minimalist haiku. Soft, diffused light spills in upon the two-story atrium-like space through an arched, coffered sandblasted glass skylight and tall casement-style windows. Colors in the room—rose, salmon, rust, celadon, teal, and stone—are the same hues as many of the delicacies on the menu. Banquettes covered in watered silk line up along the walls and face leather chairs of Italian design across the two rows of tables. Despite uncovered marble inlay floors, conversation is muted.

Prices: cup of tea, $2.50; wagashi, $4.

URASENKE CHANOYU CENTER

153 East 69th Street bet. Lexington and Third Aves.

❖ 212-988-6161

Hours: Call for schedule and reservations

The meditative, courteous Japanese tea ceremony called Chanoyu elevates the making, serving, and drinking of tea to a high art. The Tea Ceremony originated over 700 years ago; toward the end of the sixteenth century, a revered tea master, Sen No Rikkyu, established the strict code of etiquette that defines the ritual that continues to be practiced today. Chanoyu reflects four principles: Harmony, Respect, Purity, and Tranquility. Every gesture in the ceremony is choreographed to create and sustain the experience of these principles. In New York, you can experience the Tea Ceremony at the Urasenke Chanoyu Center, which was established by Dr. Shoshito Sen, a fifteenth-generation Grand Tea Master and President of the Urasenke Foundation of Kyoto. One Wednesday evening a month, from November through May, the Center hosts an introductory lecture-demonstration. Preparing to enter the tearoom is a ritual in itself. After removing their shoes, guests sit and wait, as they quietly shrug off the cares of the everyday. When summoned, they proceed into the tearoom, which is empty except for tatami mats that cover the floor, and a small, square sunken hearth, which contains a miniature stove that may be used to heat the kettle. (For the lecture, tea is prepared outside the room.) At one end of the room an elevated alcove exhibits a scroll brushed with calligraphy that expresses the theme of the ceremony, plus a simple flower arrangement meant to symbolize the fleeting beauty of nature. These are to be contemplated by the guests as they take their places. The serving of the tea, a powdered green Matcha, and an accompanying sweet, is a meditative experience, as every gesture, from the bow of thanks when offered the cup to the bow of thanks when the cup is passed from one guest to the next, is purged of gratuitous flourishes. A deep calm prevail—which, hopefully, you will carry with you when you exit the Center and reenter the outside world. The Urasenke Chanoyu Center also holds tea classes for those who wish further study in tea preparation and encourages membership in the organization to promote the understanding of Chanoyu. 73

WILD LILY TEA MARKET

545 East 12th St. bet. Aves. A and B
❖ 212-598-9097

Hours: Afternoon Tea Party 2 P.M. to 5 P.M.;
Tuesday through Sunday 11 A.M. to 10 P.M.;
Closed Mondays

Downtown in Alphabet City, the recently opened Wild Lily Tea
Market (the younger "sister" of Wild Lily Tea Room, see next
page) is fast making its presence felt. Set across from one of the
neighborhood's larger community gardens on an otherwise
unprepossessing block, the tearoom is small, like a tea box,
holding just four tiny Lucite tables. The menu, too, is short—but
sweet. Try any one of the myriad teas, all herbal, and complement
it, perhaps, with a fat scone or with a plate of cookies, which
includes a green tea cookie, "apricot windows," and a sunflower-
shaped cookie dusted with colorful crystallized sugar. Cantilevered
glass shelves display a number of blond cubic wooden boxes filled
with tea (more teas are kept in tins behind the cash register), as
well as a number of fine tea things, including a miniature jade
"aroma and drinking cup" set. A Purists' Tea Set holding a pot,
two cups, and two boxes of rare tea is a sublime gift. House tea
blends here include Rose Garden and Mint Blend, as well as the
aptly entitled Downtown Girl with Yuzu Honey.

Prices: Wild Lily Tea Market Afternoon Special: Order any $3.50 tea, and
it will be served with a scone for $6.50; scone alone, $5.25.
Cookie platter, $3.25. Boy Scout Bar pecan bar with chocolate
chips and flaked coconut, $2.75.

WILD LILY TEA ROOM

511-A West 22nd St. bet. Tenth and Eleventh Aves.
❖ 212-691-2258

Hours: Afternoon Tea Party 2 P.M. to 5 P.M.;
Tuesday through Sunday 11 A.M. to 10 P.M.;
Closed Mondays

Like a beam of light, the tiny sliver that is the Wild Lily Tea
Room pierces straight to the heart of the Chelsea art district. A
popular hangout with artists and students, the tearoom, designed
by painter Ines Sun, appears, upon entry, deceptively candid in its
demeanor; only as your eyes adjust from the outside glare do you
espy a small, perfect circle of a pool at your feet, home to two
majestic koi that dart amongst the sunbeams created by bubbles
rising to the surface of the water. Wild Lily offers over 40 teas,
each explicated with exquisite care in a handmade book whose
pages open out upon your lap like soft handkerchiefs. Many of
Wild Lily's teas sport engaging names: Popcorn is a Japanese
green tea with toasted rice and popped barley; Buddha's Finger is
made from leaves rolled to look just like that; and Chelsea Adam
is a "men's tonic" infused with a dozen herbs including energy-
boosting ginseng. Wild Lily offers a prix fixe Tea Party, served on
one-of-a-kind plates bearing exotic sandwiches such as butternut-
squash cream spread and Chinese black-tea egg salad, plus raisin-
and-apricot almond scone and velvety chocolate cake—as well as a
variety of cookies. Wild Lily Tea Room sells teas to take home, in
vacuum-sealed silver-foil packets, as well select teaware, including
a Green Tea Starter Kit, which features five kinds of tea.

Prices: prix fixe Wild Lily Tea Room Afternoon Tea Party, $21.50, pot of
tea, from $4 to $8, depending upon the rarity. Plate of assorted tea
sandwiches, $8.75. scone, green-tea tiramisu, or green-tea pound
cake with whipped cream, $5.75; take-home pound cake, $12.

Where to Buy British-Style Teaware

Setting the Table

Today the style and conventional equipage of an elegant Afternoon Tea is still much as it was in the time of Queen Victoria, when the right wares were considered essential to the enjoyment of the moment. Following are descriptions of the tea furnishings and accoutrements you might expect to find in an English country house, circa 1900. It is fun to collect any or all of these to create your own style of tea presentation.

Teapoy: a small pedestal table, often mahogany, with a lidded compartment to hold glass or lead containers for tea, and glass porcelain mixing bowls for combining special blends.

Tea caddy: a container for tea made of silver, glass, porcelain, or rare inlaid wood in an extraordinary variety of droll shapes and sizes.

Caddy spoon: a short-handled scalloped spoon used to measure tea leaves. In the early days, Chinese merchants included a scallop shell tea leaf scoop in each chest of tea they shipped to Europe.

Mote spoon: a dainty, slightly pointed spoon with a shallow or pierced bowl. It is used to skim off specks of tea leaf, which can sometimes escape from the pot into the cup.

Tea strainer: a filter designed to catch tea leaves as tea is poured into a cup. Some strainers rest over the top of the cup; others affix to the spout of the teapot, swinging over the cup as the pot is tipped to pour.

Tea kettle: Some kettles can be lifted off their metal stands, which are fitted with a burner; others are hinged to the stand so that the hostess can tip the kettle to fill the teapot. Furniture makers developed stands for this apparatus.

Tea tray: A tea tray can be almost two feet in length; it is designed to hold a kettle on its stand, a teapot, a sugar canister, tea caddies, and a milk pitcher. Such a tray might have been fashioned from solid silver, tole, or papier-mâché. Usually a tray is footed to prevent contact with wood surfaces; raised edges prevent things from sliding off.

Tea table: a small table, usually mahogany, with a carved or metal rim on which to place tea cups, spoons, and assorted tea foods. Craftsmen lavished their artistry and grace upon such tables.

Muffin dish: Made out of silver, this has a hot-water liner and high-dome lid to keep muffins warm.

Muffineer: A muffineer resembles a large-scale domed pepper pot with a perforated decorative top. It is used to sprinkle cinnamon or sugar on toasted goodies.

Toasting fork: a long handled, two- or three-tined, spindly fork made out of wrought iron with a wooden handle. It was intended to hold a bread slice or crumpet at arms length over the open fire so that you did not burn yourself.

Sugar basin: a basin used to hold pieces of sugar broken off from a cone. (You can still find sugar sold in heavy cones.) Sugar tongs then permitted guests to pick up their sugar and drop it into the cup.

Slop bowl: a bowl in which to pour the dregs of the prior cup of tea.

Teacup: a shallow, gently swelling bowl with a single handle, from which tea is sipped. Some teacups are also footed. When the first handleless tea bowls arrived from the Orient, European ladies found them extremely uncomfortable to hold in the hand. Thus, by the mid-1750s, teacups with handles appeared.

Saucer: a shallow plate with a circular indentation into which is set the teacup. The saucer also has a shallow lip to prevent the cup from slipping off, and acts as an impromptu spoon rest. It was once considered acceptable to pour your tea into the saucer and sip it—some elderly British folk still do so.

Creamer: a small pitcher for milk, either matching the tea china or of silver or other metal. The name is a misnomer, since cream should never be put in tea—its high fat content masks the flavor and oil globules may float on top.

Teaspoon: a pointed or oval spoon used for blending milk and dissolving sugar into tea. Decorative, shallow-bowled, oval teaspoons usually come in sets of six, eight, or twelve—or they might form part of a complete cutlery service. In the hierarchy of spoons, they come after the dessert and before the coffee spoon. The Victorians enjoyed novelty and souvenir teaspoons. Today teaspoons can be collected one-by-one to make mismatched sets.

–Veronica McNiff

Shops & Boutiques

AGES PAST

450 East 78th St. bet. York and First Aves.

❖ 212-628-0725

Hours: Monday through Saturday 11 A.M. to 5 P.M.,
        but call ahead

A tiny clapboard nineteenth-century shopfront suggests a
Connecticut seafaring town—Stonington, possibly. Inside, Ages
Past is a repository of gentle nineteenth-century charm of the
most rarefied kind: brilliant yellow canary ware, pink lustre, early
Wedgwood, early to mid-Victorian English china. This is the place
to discover transfer ware, too. In the eighteenth century, potters
learned how to apply quaint and sometimes moral decorative
scenes and mottos directly onto the china. While this may have
been a technological novelty—or a way to save money—the result-
ing ceramics make charming tea collectibles, though you might
want to save them for special occasions, like royalty coming to
tea. In that case, Ages Past could assist you with commemorative
tea things, a deft way to flatter a monarchical ego. These are a
specialty here. Some of them are of very early time periods and
correspondingly expensive but there are lots of affordable ones
from the last two or three generations of Windsors.

BARDITH LTD.

901 Madison Ave. at 72nd St.
❖ 212-737-3775
31 E. 72nd St. bet. Madison and Park Aves.
❖ 212-737-8660
Hours: Monday through Friday 11 A.M. to 5:30 P.M.

While waiting for the M2 Limited bus at 72nd Street and
Madison, peruse the ravishing porcelains and other treasures visi-
ble through Bardith's windows. Inside, shelves and étagères are
crammed with exquisite examples of the late seventeenth- to mid-
nineteenth-century English, Continental, and Chinese porcelains,
delft, faïence, and period glass. You may simply want to hold your
breath with delight at their beauty—and terror lest you accidentally
brush against something irreplaceable. Is it a coincidence that
store personnel are slim and agile as eels? Bardith on Madison
sells full-size and rare miniature tea pots, partial tea sets, and single cups and saucers. The dozens of papier-mâché trays dating
from the turn of the nineteenth century onward represent the
city's best collection. Sequestered round the corner on East 72nd
Street is a seraglio of complete tea sets. Scrolled in gold and indigo, lushly bouquet'd on gilt grounds, sprigged, dotted, striped, or
swagged, these delicious creations require checks written with
many zeros. Bardith also sells fine furnishings at this location.

BARNEYS CHELSEA PASSAGE

660 Madison Ave. bet. 60th and 61st Sts.

❖ 212-826-8900

Hours: Monday through Friday 10 A.M. to 8 P.M.;
      Saturday 10 A.M. to 7 P.M.;
      Sunday 11 A.M. to 6 P.M.

Barneys has devoted much of its entire second floor–The Chelsea Passage–to adorning the home with objects and artifacts that represent the cutting edge in rarefied taste. One bank of shelves, for example, is dedicated to JARS, a manufacturer of luminescent crackle-glazed wares that include some of the most tantalizing tea pots in town; colors appear as evanescent as air and sea. Another wall displays the work of Sophie Villepique, whose wares shimmer with a pearly luster. Yet another case contains a whimsical Miro-like teapot that sports an elephant trunk-shaped spout; there are fat cups to match. Kettles also receive their due: The Chelsea Passage carries the Alessi line, including the classic Whistling Bird by architect Michael Graves. A mini-boutique of Fauchon teas, jams, and crystallized sugar sticks, an alcove of fine linens, and a corner shop where you can monogram invitations enrich the Barneys shopping experience.

BERGDORF GOODMAN

754 Fifth Ave. bet. 58th and 59th Sts.

❖ 212-753-7300

Hours: Monday through Saturday 10 A.M. to 6 P.M.;
Thursday 10 A.M. to 8 P.M.; Sunday Noon to 6 P.M.

The epitome of luxurious chic, Bergdorf's seventh floor is Seventh
Heaven for tea savant-collectors. Step off the up escalator into
their entrancing Vintage Tea Shop, the first in an enticing
sequence of linked, lushly carpeted and richly stocked rooms
devoted to hotel silver, fine linens, porcelain, and crystal. Along
your path are mini room and table settings to inspire you to
greater flights of fancy in your own home. You would have far to
go to find a better selection of distinguished antique, vintage, and
retro teaware. Complete and partial tea services are displayed in
bright vitrines, while a central table and an array of towel bars,
baskets and caddies hoard tea towels and cozies as well as irresistible caches of exquisite silver serving pieces, including pastry
tongs. For those who adore serving tea to friends in mismatched
cups, one tall étagère highlights a collection of individual speci-
mens in a variety of sizes and shapes. On a recent visit, one-of-a-
kind items included a delicately engraved English sterling silver
biscuit box dating from 1880 and a pair of funky shell-shaped lusterware tea-and-toast sets from the 1930s. Everything in the
Vintage Tea Shop is in mint condition—not a chip or crack anywhere.

BERNARDAUD

499 Park Ave. bet. 56th an 57th Sts.

❖ 212-371-4300

Hours: Monday through Friday 10 A.M. to 7 P.M.;
        Saturday 10 A.M. to 6 P.M.;
        Closed Sunday

This elegant repository of French porcelains, which relocated from Madison to Park Avenue, has set aside an intimate space within their flagship store to showcase all things related to the service of tea. Amongst the panoply of wares, sterling silver tea infusers and a curvy caddy in Bernardaud's signature "Galerie Royale" pale jade and white stripe pattern stand out. Olivier Gagnere, the designer of the caddy—and myriad other teawares—masterminded the design of the shop as well, and it shows in telling details, such as the plushy sofas that invite the shopper (or the shopper's spouse) to linger awhile and enjoy the atmosphere. Bernardaud also carries a selection of 14 leaf teas, including Ceylon O.P. Pettigalia, Verte a la Menthe, and caramel tea. These, too, are packaged in "Galerie Royale" tins. Bernardaud's own assortment of jams and condiments might be served in a dainty little Limoges jam pot. Galerie Royale boxed sets are also available: Check out the canister and tea package; it would make a lovely gift.

BE-SPECKLED TROUT

422 Hudson St. bet. Morton St. and St. Luke's Pl.

❖ 212-255-1421

Hours: Monday through Saturday 10 A.M. to 8 P.M.;
Sunday 10 A.M. to 7 P.M.

Packed to the gills with one-of-a-kind finds from mittel Europa to
the icy reaches of northern Wisconsin, the Be-Speckled Trout is
replete with friendly and fanciful old tea things: antique tea cups
and saucers sold one by one to mix and match, arcane angling
and fishing antiques (flies hand-tied a generation ago in England
are still pristine in their maker's tin cases), jokey small novelties,
and lodge-type souvenirs easy on the pocket. The Trout is located
next to Anglers & Writers (see page 24), also owned by Craig
Bero, and represents the owner's recollections of his grandfather
general store back home in Algoma, Wisconsin. It is a successful
and charming distillation of those childhood memories. Spied
from the sidewalk, the modest, multipaned shop front reveals elusive glimpses of tea pots, each as distinctive a personality and
shape as village women gathered to gossip. Beyond, there is the
promising impression of Hoosier-style oak cabinets, crowded
shelves, and glass-fronted wooden counters laden with inviting
objects. Baked goods tempt from an old glass cabinet and there
are Mariage Frères and Harney & Sons teas in tins or sold
loose by weight.

FORTUNOFF

681 Fifth Ave. bet. 53rd and 54th Sts.

❖ 212-758-6660

Hours: Monday through Saturday 10 A.M. to 6 P.M;
Thursday until 7 P.M.

Just up the street from New York's diamond market, Fortunoff's glitzy 1970s-style store is touted as a major resource for vintage estate teaware. Zip past banked trays of sparkling rings to find the elevator and take this to the fourth floor. Put on your dark glasses before stepping out onto the red carpet and slinking past the chromed pillars that hold up the soaring ceiling. The silver, densely displayed on spotlit glass shelves backed with mirror, can only be described as staggering. The dozens of partial and full tea services on view may include trays; the style runs the gamut from robber-baron late Victoriana to Edwardian effete or Forties funky.

JAMES II GALLERIES, LTD.

11 East 57th St. bet. Fifth and Madison Aves.

❖ 212-355-7040

Hours: Monday through Friday 10 A.M. to 5:30 P.M.;
Saturday 10:30 A.M. to 5 P.M; Closed Sunday

Suitably located on East 57th Street, James II is a decorative arts collector's idea of paradise. Owner Barbara Munves celebrates the nineteenth century's delight in confident color and pattern with verve and the two floors are packed to bursting with finds for the well-dressed tea table. Precious things include tea caddies galore, fashioned in Georgian cut glass, silver, shagreen, and papier-mâché; sardine boxes (a feature of the fashionable Victorian table); biscuit barrels; jampots; strainers; tea kettles large and small, both silver and plated; full and partial tea sets; dessert plates; and much, much more. Don't overlook the rare Victorian miniature tea sets, or the 1930s metal-mounted ceramic tea trays and extraordinary sandwich boxes handled like evening bags.

JAMES ROBINSON

480 Park Ave. at 58th St.

❖ 212-752-6166

Hours: Monday through Saturday 10 A.M. to 5 P.M.

James Robinson is just the place to go for a Georgian mote spoon—used to lift out the small tea leaves that sometimes shoot the teapot rapids into your cup. Restrained ideas about window display reaffirm its role as one of the city's most respected resources for Georgian silver, dazzling English and Continental dining and tea service porcelains (look for intact gilt), and antique jewelry. The firm's dignified persona and status is further expressed through its spacious Park Avenue premises decorously upholstered in library green, and punctuated with mahogany glass fronted cases. In these you will find sugar nippers, tea strainers, sugar casters, silver and glass jampots—all the antique accoutrements of civilized tea-drinking. Massive double doors at the rear of the store open to reveal a veritable silver vault, where tea pots and coffeepots stand in serried ranks, along with tea caddies, cream jugs, and sugar bowls. If you are a connoisseur looking for a rare (and costly) octagonal George III teapot, start here. If you like and can afford very good tea things, James Robinson offers modern replicas, hand-hammered from a solid sheet of silver in the eighteenth-century manner.

LA TERRINE

1024 Lexington Ave. at 73rd St.
❖ 212-988-3366
Hours: Monday through Saturday 10:30 A.M. to 6 P.M.

Like a diorama of a nineteenth-century potter's shop, La Terrine
floor-to-ceiling shelving displays tightly packed, colorful ceramics.
Everything you could ever want for the table can be seen at a
glance from the sidewalk. Beautifully painted traditional artisan
wares from Portugal, Italy, Brazil, and France crowd right up to
the windows, pushing one another out of the way. Tea pots with
perky knobbed lids come in all shapes, patterns, and sizes; you
can create full or partial sets item by item. If you cannot splurge
right now, dodge around the massive columns that represent an
obstacle course in maneuvering around the store, to award yourself just one of the individually painted mugs hanging from pegs.
Natural wood walls and fixtures, paper packing "straw" cushioning
the teetering piles of plates, and the cartons that always seem to
have just been delivered from some continental point of origin,
give La Terrine an informal feeling. There are stacks of vibrant
Provençal and toile, tablecloths, placemats and napkins to
pillage as well.

MAYA SCHAPER CHEESE AND ANTIQUES

106 West 69th St. bet. Columbus Ave. and Broadway
❖ 212-873-2100
Hours: Daily 10 A.M. to 8 P.M.

A fastidiously simple store where cheese from around the world peacefully coexists with culinary antiques and fine teas, Maya Schaper's is redolent of charm rather than brie. Schaper hunts down tea and dining wares on regular trips to Europe, carrying home with her as much as she can by hand. The exquisitely edited selection of antique and vintage wares, which date from about 1830 to 1940, change all the time and are displayed on old-fashioned wire shelving on your right as you enter the store. On any given day, expect to find old English Hovis brand bread pans; bread boards with wood-handled knives; complete and partial tea sets and dessert plates, painted, as was the ladylike fashion of the time, by Victorian women in need of an artistic hobby; cake stands; cut-glass jampots; and silver serving pieces and cutlery. In all, quite a culinary compendium. There are also attractively packaged teas for sale. At the back, and in the downstairs gallery, you will find old pine and painted furniture.

WILLIAM-WAYNE & COMPANY

850 Lexington Ave. bet. 64th and 65th Sts.

❖ 212-288-9243

846 Lexington Ave. bet. 64th and 65th Sts.

❖ 212-737-8934

Hours: Monday through Saturday 10:30 A.M. to 6:30 P.M.

40 University Pl. at 9th St.

❖ 212-533-4711

Hours: Monday through Saturday 11 A.M. to 7 P.M.;
Sunday 1 P.M. to 6 P.M.

William-Wayne's witty sensibility and eclectic mix of home accessories—along with the framed prints of impish monkeys always in
residence—guarantees the three stores (two are side-by-side) a place
in the city's pantheon of shopping resources. Stroll in to examine
the charming displays, full of decorating ideas. Look for the
antique teasets, pretty mugs, Victorian cutlery such as bread forks
and jam spoons—and Victorian lemonade pitchers ideal for iced tea
to create your teatime setting. There are tea tables old and new,
custom-made chairs, and decorative pillows to sink back into with
your cup of tea. Select one of fifteen handsome open stock
Limoges or Spode china patterns for your bridal list (if you have
here, givers might get inspired).

Where to Buy Tea

RETAIL SHOPS

The following are some of the retail shops around town that carry fine teas and tea things. Some will fulfill orders by mail, or over the 'Net. Check!

ALICE'S TEA CUP

102 West 73rd St. bet. Columbus and Amsterdam Aves.
❖ 212-799-3006
Hours: Tuesday through Friday 11:30 A.M. to 8 P.M.;
Saturday 10:30 A.M. to 10 P.M.;
Sunday 11 A.M. to 8 P.M.; Closed Monday.

Just inside the front door of Alice's Tea Cup (see page 23) is the tearoom's unpretentious shop, which features a selection of tea pots and cozies, as well a wall of giant tins containing the 112 (and counting) teas that Alice's also offers on its tantalizing eat-in menu. Tea prices, based on one ounce of loose tea, range from about $1.50 to about $13.75, the latter being the 1-oz. price of Japanese Gyokuro green tea. Some exotics hail from Africa: of particular note is Cameroon Fannings, a tea grown in a volcano 3,300 feet above sea level. Pricey rare teas include Drink Me Detox Blend and Silver Needle Jasmine, both white teas, and an oolong called Bai Hao White Tip Champagne Oolong. For a green tea called Finest Jasmine Pearls, green-tea leaves are rolled together with fine jasmine buds. Alice's eponymous blend mingles Indian black and Japanese green teas with rose petals. Ten of Alice's teas are also available at their chic little outpost—The Mad Tea Cup—located on the third floor of the Burberry's boutique on East 57th Street (see page 47).

BODUM CAFÉ & HOMESTORE

413-415 West 14th St. bet. Ninth and Tenth Aves.

❖ 212-367-9125

Hours: Monday through Saturday 10 A.M. to 7 P.M.;
Sunday Noon to 6 P.M.

Bodum's master designer Carsten Jorgenson is the creator of the
company's hugely popular Bistro plunger-style coffee press, which
was introduced in 1974. Applying the Bistro principle of squeez-
ing the essence out of coffee grinds to tea leaves, Jorgensen came
up with a series of tea presses, including the chummy spherical
Assam and Shin Cha pots (the latter has a longer spout). Made of
glass, each press is designed with a removable infuser, plus a
plunger built into its lid; once the tea has brewed to the desired
strength, simply push the plunger into the infuser to press every
iota of intensity from the leaves—and to stop further brewing.
Bodum also carries an array of stovetop and electric kettles,
including the dimpled Ottoni, and the Osiris, originally designed
for MoMA's museum shop. Two handy-dandy little devices caught
our fancy, one a milk frother (with companion glass mug), the
other, a one-cup infuser and glass mug set called the YoYo.
Bodum's 100 teas—which hail from Asia and Africa—occupy one
wall. Thirty-five are blacks and 15 are greens. Most of the rest
are fruit teas or herbals, some of which contain as many as a
dozen different aromas and essences. All are sold in 200-gram
packages. (See also page 43 for a description of Bodum's tea bar.)

CARRY ON AT TEA ℛ SYMPATHY

108-110 Greenwich Ave. bet. 12th and 13th Sts.

❖ 212-807-8329

Hours: Monday through Saturday 11 A.M. to 10:30 P.M.,
Sunday 11 A.M. to 10 P.M.

Sandwiched between Tea ℛ Sympathy's tearoom (see page 37)
and their fish-and-chips shop, A Salt and Battery, Carry On, quite
literally, does carry on—the tradition of Jolly Olde England—and
tea. Carry On's shelves are fairly bursting with teapots, teakettles,
teaware, teas, condiments, and candies. Here you'll find the
Chatsford teapot in a dozen cheery hues, some novelty tea pots, a
wide assortment of mugs, and tins of teas (in a mix of sizes) from
the likes of Ty-Phoo, P.G.Tips, Yorkshire Gold, and Ahmad.
Moving from shelves to countertop, windowsill, and display rack
and the merch gets wilder—a sort of freefall into British telly
humor: Union Jack thongs and loo rolls, videos of some of the
U.K.'s favorite shows—etc., etc.—plus touristy take-aways, such as
notecards shaped like London double-decker buses, phone booths
and, of course, tea pots. Carry On also provides a local takeout
service, which is especially welcome because, as everyone in the
neighborhood knows, Tea ℛ Sympathy's tiny tearoom does not
accept reservations. The menu includes a Tea Time repast of tea
sandwiches, scone with jam and clotted cream, cake, biscuits, and
tea bags for two. (Carry On will not deliver hot tea.) Be sure to
take note of the tearoom's memoir, *Tea ℛ Sympathy: The Life
of an English Tea Shop in New York* written by Anita Naughton
with owner Nicola Perry. If you can't get into the tearoom, you,
too, can carry on—by whipping up one of the book's 60 recipes.

CHELSEA MARKET BASKETS

75 Ninth Ave. bet. 15th and 16th Sts.

❖ 212-727-1111

Hours: Monday through Friday 9:30 A.M. to 7:30 P.M.,
         Saturday 10 A.M. to 7:30 P.M.; Sunday 10 A.M. to 6 P.M.

The vast, sprawling block of warehouses moated by Ninth and
Tenth Avenues and 15th and 16th Streets is a raw-boned repository for a veritable cornucopia of flowers and foodstuffs. Snaking
your way through the interconnected buildings is an exercise in
self-restraint; why not, after all, sampling a soup here, a snack
there? For packaged teas, head straight for Chelsea Market
Baskets. A charming emporium-within-an-emporium, the shop col-
lects and sells delicacies that are decidedly not mainstays of a diet:
instead you will find all sorts of tempting delights, from candies to
condiments. The expanded tea department in the shop includes a
new line-up of 30 bulk, loose-leaf teas by Harney ℜ Sons and
Ahmad; these can be purchased by the ounce. Some of London-
based Ahmad's boxed and tinned teas, sold separately, are ear-
marked for specific times of day such as afternoon or evening.
True to its name, and as the company's lavishly illustrated catalog
proves (www.ChelseaMarketBaskets.com; 888-727-7887),
Chelsea Market Baskets specializes in assembling gift baskets for
every gustatory persuasion. The Afternoon Tea hamper, for example, contains a mind-boggling array of scrumptious British-made
treats, including crumpets and shortbread, lemon curd, raisin
scone mix, clotted cream, jam, and two teas, Ahmad's Afternoon
Tea and a fruit tea (in bags). The Tea Emporium hamper holds
three loose-leaf teas from Rishi-Teas (Maghreb Mint, Organic Earl
Grey, and Serene Chamomile), a glass pitcher, gold-filtered brewing cup, shortbread, and ginger cookies, plus Belgian chocolates
from Dolfin—all wrapped in a tea towel.

CRABTREE & EVELYN, LTD

1310 Madison Ave. at 93rd St.
❖ 212-289-3923
520 Madison Ave. bet. 53rd and 54th Sts., Shop #5
❖ 212-758-6419
620 Fifth Ave. at Rockefeller Center ❖ 212-581-5022
Staten Island Mall, 2655 Richmond Ave. ❖ 718-982-8252
Hours: Vary according to location

Mail order:
P. O. Box 187
Woodstock Hill, CT 02681
❖ 800-272-2873
www.crabtree-evelyn.com

Founded by Cyrus Harvey, Crabtree & Evelyn pays tribute to the
philosophy of one John Evelyn, a noted seventeenth-century
English conservationist, who introduced the first olive-oil salad
dressing to England. Today, Crabtree & Evelyn markets dozens
of flower, fruit, and herb-scented products for the home, as well as
a luscious array of teas, jams, cookies, shortbreads, and biscuits.
As reported in our First Edition, one of our favorite spreads is a
delicious lemon curd packaged in C&E's signature octagonal jar—
which then can be recycled into a juice glass, or used to store any-
thing from preserves to push pins. Upon request, Crabtree &
Evelyn will wrap gifts, gratis.

DEAN & DELUCA

560 Broadway bet. Prince and Spring Sts.

New York, NY 10012

❖ 212-431-1691

Hours: Monday through Saturday 10 A.M. to 8 P.M.;
        Sunday 10 A.M. to 7 P.M.

Mail Order:

2526 East 36th St. North Circle

Wichita, KS 67219

❖ 800-221-7714

www.deandeluca.com

This Soho-based emporium of fine foods is revered by anyone who cooks—or pretends to. The range of comestibles and potables on view on the full-to-bursting shelves is exhaustive, and perhaps even intimidating to the uninitiated. Teas are collected on a tall Metro shelf at the center of the store, and include the usual suspects, as well as fancier imports such as Mariages Frères. Dean & Deluca also stocks a number of tea pots and kettles, as well as their own chunky, diner-style logo-emblazoned mugs. The mail-order catalog and website, which are updated frequently, devote several pages to tea and tea things. A recent catalog cover featured a D&D exclusive, the lustrous retro-styled, earth-hued Heath Teapot, made in California. D&D invites tea aficionados to join their Tea Continuity Program, which highlights a different tea each month. Some of these teas are exclusive to them, while others are specialty brews by some of their suppliers, such as Red & Green, Grace Tea, and Kusmi. You can join for three or six months, or for a full year. Recent gift packages included the Proustian Salon de Thé, complete with a fat Pillivuyt teapot, a tea tray, and teas from Hediard, Berry Bros, and Kusmi—plus a jar of marmalade, a box of chocolate feuilettes and a tin of, yes, petite madeleines.

ELI'S VINEGAR FACTORY

431 East 91st St. bet. First and York Aves.

❖ 212-987-0885

Hours: Daily 7 A.M. to 9 P.M.; upstairs dining level,
        Weekend brunch only, 8 A.M. to 4 P.M.

Eli Zabar appears to be the baker to us all. Everywhere you look, there's an Eli's truck delivering its robust breads and scrumptious baked goods. And, yes, Virginia, there is an Eli (son of the original Zabar) as well as an Eli's bakery, way east on one of those forsaken blocks of the upper Upper East Side occupied by car rental agencies, moving van companies, and limo services. Taking advantage of an opportunity to broaden his horizons in this otherwise under-endowed area of Manhattan, Eli took over a rundown vinegar factory just down 91st Street from his bakery and converted it into a bustling marketplace-cum-eatery. Entering by way of the VF's swinging doors—giant flaps really—you are thrust right smack into sensory overload, for Eli carries virtually everything you might ever want to cook and/or eat, from trout to truffles. Teas are conveniently clustered near the honeys, for those who prefer this sweetener to sugar. The VF carries a dozen Eli blends, which you can sniff and scoop yourself; pay for these by the quarter pound. Flavors include a brain-clearing Yunnan China Black, smoky Russian Caravan, and an assortment of herbals, including a rooibos. Fortnum & Mason bring to jaded New Yorkers a specialty brew blended just for us called New York. Look, too, for Chi for Life, an herbal with 10 vitamins. In the cookware section of the store, you will find hefty cast-iron kettles by Lodge, OXO's arthritis-friendly Good Grips kettle with ergonomic handle, and Cuisine Cookware's hotel/professional stainless-steel kettle. T-Sacs filters are sold here, too. At the back of the store is a tea and coffee bar; here the early morning crowd lines up to pour their own before hopping the express busses that shuttle them to their offices downtown.

ELI'S MANHATTAN

1411 Third Ave. bet 80th and 81st Sts.

❖ 212-717-8100

Hours: Daily 7 A.M. to 9 P.M.

Eli's Third Avenue operation fills a basement and part of the street floor of a former moving and storage warehouse with most of the same foods and housewares as the Vinegar Factory. Lighter and brighter than its 91st Street sibling, Eli's Manhattan is easier to negotiate, but you have to carry your purchases up an escalator to the checkout. A few additions to the tea lineup stand out, such as Bewley's of Ireland Irish Afternoon, Golden Moon's herbals such as Honey Pear, and Hediard's robust teas in their distinctive red tins. Eli's Manhattan also carries Brooke Bond PG Tips pyramidal tea bags. Ditto a range of tea pots.

EMPIRE COFFEE & TEA COMPANY

568 Ninth Ave. bet. 41st and 42nd Sts.
❖ 212-268-1220 or 800-262-5908
Hours: Weekdays 8 A.M. to 7 P.M.;
　　　　Saturday 9 A.M. to 6:30 P.M.;
　　　　Sunday 11 A.M. to 5 P.M.

This no-frills, family-run operation has zigzagged within a five-block radius in Hell's Kitchen since its opening in 1908. It recently moved again—one block south of its former location—but is still on Food Road within steps of Port Authority and close enough to the theater district to make it a tempting stop-off for commuters and matinee mavens. Bulk teas number almost six dozen, ranging from blacks to scented flavors. Boxed bags include some unusual blends: Angel Blend Flu-Fighter, for one, as well as Traditional Medicine's American GinZing and Breezy Morning's Nite Cap—for nerves and insomnia—and Uncle Lee's Body Slim Dieter Tea with a tapemeasured waistline illustrated on its box top. Empire sells a kettle and a classic white porcelain teapot as well as a few mugs.

FAUCHON, INC.

442 Park Ave. at 56th St. ❖ 212-308-5919

1000 Madison Ave. bet. 77th and 78th Sts.

❖ 212-570-2211

Hours: Monday through Friday 7:30 A.M. to 7 P.M.;
       Saturday 9 A.M. to 7 P.M.;
       Sunday 10 A.M. to 6 P.M.

Fauchon has been purveying fine and rare teas for over a century, since its founding in Paris in 1886 by August Fauchon. In New York, Fauchon offers over 100 teas, including blacks, greens, and oolongs as well as over two dozen flavored herbal tisanes. A handy brochure at the tea counter elucidates the particulars of each tea, and helpfully categorizes them by the time of day they might be most enjoyed: all-day, morning, afternoon, and/or evening. The brochure also counsels optimum brewing times for each type. Teas are packaged in a variety of ways. Our favorites are the handy little travel tins, each of which holds five crystal tea sachets made of microfiber; flavors are three—Earl Grey, Apple, and a Fauchon exclusive called Soir de France. These and other teas are also available in boxes of 15 or 25 tea bags and in bulk boxes. The largest container holds 500 grams, or 17.60 oz., of tea. Three types of crystallized sugar sticks, two dark and one white, are poised nearby to stir into the tea of your choice. Fauchon is, of course, best known for its sumptuous array of candies, condiments, and other delicacies, and the New York venues do not disappoint. Here you'll find Parisian specialties, such as marron glaces, marzipan veggies, and chewy pate de fruits, as well as cookies and patisseries of every delectable description. Gift packaging, be it a box or tin, is irresistible. (To learn about taking tea at either Fauchon, please see page 31.)

GOURMET GARAGE

453 Broome St. at Mercer St.

❖ 212-941-5850

117 Seventh Ave. at 10th St.

❖ 212-699-5980

301 East 64th St. bet. First and Second Aves.

❖ 212-535-6271

2567 Broadway at 96th St.

❖ 212-663-0656

Hours: Monday through Saturday 8 A.M. to 9 P.M.;
          Sunday 8 A.M. to 8 P.M.

Delivery Service: 10 A.M. to 7 P.M.

E-mail for deliveries: GGatHome@aol.com.

Shop Like a Chef! So proclaims the Gourmet Garage—and so you can. Meccas for fanatical cooks, the four Garages do just what they say: "garage" mouth-watering gourmet goodies, both packaged and fresh. Teas and tisanes here have been conscientiously selected to enhance your health. So-called Traditional Medicinals, for example, include PMS Tea, Throat Coat, infused with licorice and slippery elm, plus Cold Care PM and Breathe Easy, which presume to relieve congestion and help you sleep. T42 teas, fruit blends all, include raspberry, mango, lemon, and strawberry. A brand called Assam leans on more eco-sensitive names; check out Haarlem Honeybunch or Community Green. Oregon chai come in versions labeled original and spiced versions, as well as a latte mix, which is a black tea flavored with honey, vanilla, and spices. Gourmet Garage also sells gift baskets; East Side Tea Time is packed to bursting with jam, marmalade, and honey, plus cinnamon sugar almonds, a chocolate bar, butter wafers and ladyfingers; teas in the basket are a Vanilla Almond blend from Republic of Tea and a Scottish Breakfast from Taylor's of Harrowgate.

GRACE'S MARKETPLACE

1237 Third Ave. at 71st St.

❖ 212-737-0600

Hours: Monday through Saturday 7 A.M. to 8:30 P.M.;
Sunday 8 A.M. to 7 P.M.

The tea section in this always-crowded Upper East Side fine-foods
emporium is slightly overwhelmed by the coffees, but, not to
worry, you will find a nice selection of teas here, to whit: Grace's
Rare Teas (no relation) in large and small tins; Dr. Stuart's
herbals, including a Valerian Plus; Stash, including a Triple
Ginseng for those who feel particularly depleted; Pompadour;
+AZO; and Kusmi. Green teas are represented by and Sushi Chef
Japanese green tea, and by Darly. Even Salada makes one. Check
out the go-withs while you are here, too; Grace's stocks an array
of bakery goods as well as honeys and preserves.

M. ROHRS' HOUSE OF FINE TEAS AND COFFEES

303 East 85th St. bet. First and Second Aves.
New York, NY 10028
❖ 212-396-4456
Hours: Monday through Wednesday 6 A.M. to 9:30 P.M., Thursday
through Saturday 10 A.M. to 9:30 P.M., Closed Sunday

This little hole-in-the-wall on the Upper East Side dispenses over 90 varieties of loose-leaf tea—hard to believe when you consider that whatever space there is is shared not only with coffees, but with a selection of pre-packaged teas and teaware, as well as honeys, candies, jams, and fresh rugalach. If you drop in often enough for a take-away cup of tea (or coffee)—at least six times—you can pick up a "complimentary drink card" that gives you the seventh cup free. While you are at it, flip the card and read about the 12 qualities Rohrs' claim may be found in every cup of their coffee (and presumably tea, as well): loyalty, obedience, love, cooperation, faith, respect, honesty, compassion, mercy, persistence, peace, and—finally—self-control. That's a proper recipe for life, too, don't you think? Rohrs' will also make up gift baskets upon request. If you order one, ask them to enclose one of the cards.

MYERS OF KESWICK

634 Hudson St. bet. Horatio and Jane Sts.

❖ 212-691-4194

Hours: Monday through Friday 10 A.M. to 7 P.M.;

          Saturday 10 A.M. to 6 P.M.;

          Sunday Noon to 5 P.M.

Keswick is a town in the English Lake District, and that is where Mr. Myers himself comes from. His shop is the kind of genial down-to-earth grocer's store that is not so easy to find even in England anymore. Its décor depends upon the shopkeeper's pride and glory of meticulously tidy shelves of homey provender, not the phony kind like Gentlemen's Relish. Come Christmas, Myers is thronged with the nostalgia-prone Anglophiles who cannot go on any longer without their Smarties, McVities' Chocolate Digestives, Twiglets, and Cumberland sausages. Date-stamped English Ty-Phoo and P.G. Tips are also available. These are the teas that got the British through the blitz: they brew up fast and strong, and are drunk with milk and plenty of sugar. Churchill drank gallons in the Whitehall War Room. Mr. Myers makes the lemon curd tarts, pork pies, and bangers himself. Don't miss the tea cozies hand-knit by two Keswick ladies.

OREN'S DAILY ROAST

31 Waverly Place bet. University Pl. and Greene St.

❖ 212-420-5958

434 Third Ave. bet. 30th and 31st Sts.

❖ 212-779-1241

33 East 58th St. bet. Madison and Park Aves.

❖ 212-838-3345

985 Lexington Ave. at 71st St.

❖ 212-717-3907

1144 Lexington Ave. bet. 79th and 80th Sts.

❖ 212-472-6830

1574 First Ave. bet. 81st and 82nd Sts. ❖ 212-737-2690

Plus Grand Central Terminal and Penn Station, on the
LIRR Concourse Level

Hours: Monday through Friday 7 A.M. to 7 P.M.;
Saturday 10 A.M. to 6 P.M.;
Sunday 10 A.M. to 5 P.M.

Like a friendly Labrador, the aromatic blast of roasting coffee
almost knocks you over as you enter any one of the cozy Oren's
Daily Roasts. While it is true that "coffee is the heart of Oren's,"
there are over two dozen black, oolong, flavored, and decaf loose
teas for sale in every shop, safely cached in airtight glass jars.
Packaged teas are represented by The Republic of Tea, Barrow's,
and Alexander's. Tea accessories include a small but discriminating selection of porcelain and cast-iron tea pots, as well as some
clay Yixing tea pots from China. Tea balls, strainers, and mugs are
also available here.

PORTO RICO IMPORTING COMPANY

50 Grove St. bet. Seventh Ave. and West 4th St.

❖ 212-633-9453

107 Thompson St. bet. Prince and Spring Sts.

❖ 212-966-5758

201 Bleecker St. bet. Sixth Ave. and McDougal St.

❖ 212-477-5421

40 St. Mark's Place. bet. First and Second Aves.

❖ 212-533-1982

Hours: Monday through Saturday 9 A.M. to 9 P.M.;
         Sunday Noon to 7 P.M.

With its back-to-basics décor and no-nonsense service, Porto Rico delivers what it promises—over six dozen loose-leaf teas of every type, displayed in tea tins, as well as coffee beans in huge burlap sacks. To witness the daily line-up, it is the quality of tea that counts here, not pinkie-in-the-air niceties. A complete line of brewing accoutrements is as carefully selected as the variety of teas themselves. The assortment of tea pots ranges from whimsical ceramics to traditional Brown Bettys to Japanese cast-irons. Bagged teas are also available—note +AZO, Bewely's, Fortnum & Mason, Benchley's, and Twinings—as well as iced teas and chai. Flavorings include Torani flavored syrups.

ZABAR'S

2245 Broadway bet. 80th and 81st Sts.
❖ 212-787-2000 or 212-426-1234
Hours: Monday through Saturday 9 A.M. to 7 P.M.;
         Sundays 9 A.M. to 6 P.M.

Generations of New Yorkers have grown up with Zabar's as the
place to go for wonderful cheeses, great deli foodstuffs, baked
goods, and prepared foods. Exotic imported foods overpopulate
the miles of shelves, and there is an ever-seething conga line of
hungry foodies to be found snaking its way through Zabar's con-
gested aisles. Teas are arrayed on a tall Metro shelf within arm's
reach of all the yummy cookies, tea breads, and rugalachs your
heart (and stomach) may desire. Nearby are honeys and sugars.
The tea selection includes Fortnum & Mason, Kusmi-Teas (created in St. Petersburg in 1867, and now purveyed in muslin tea
bags, in boxes and tins), Barrows Japanese green tea, Dr. Stuart's
herbals, and +AZOs including Envy and Om, and Zen organic
greens. Also represented are Hu-kwa and Ty-Phoo as well as the
ubiquitous Twining and Bigelow. Upstairs, on the mezzanine level,
you can find everything for the practical kitchen—and that includes
literally dozens of styles of kettles and tea pots, as well as mugs,
strainers, and thermal carafes. A few brands to note: Krups,
DeLonghi, and Chef's Choice for cordless kettles, and Le Creuset,
Copco, All-Clad, Revere, and Bonjour for standard types. Zabar's
also carries Bodum's Ceylon Ice Tea Maker, and, for purists
loathe to brew their tea with NYC tap water, a water filter with a
10-year warranty that fits right over the faucet, by Pür.

MAIL ORDER & WEBSITES

There are literally dozens, if not hundreds, of websites that pertain to tea and teawares. Following is an extremely short list of some of these sites; the letters (MO) indicate that the operation also sends out a mail-order catalog or flyer.

THE CHARLESTON TEA PLANTATION (MO)

6617 Maybank Hwy. Wadmalaw Island, SC 29487

❖ 800-443-5987

For tours of the plantation, if you are in the area:

❖ 803-559-0383

America's only native-grown tea, aptly named America's Classic Tea, is cultivated on an island that lies not far from the gracious city of Charleston, South Carolina. The plantation's first-flush tea, harvested in May and offered in a limited edition, is available each year while supplies last; other blends are offered all year round. Harvest runs from May through October; daily tours, by appointment only, can be taken during this time. Teas come bagged, loose, or packaged with jelly, honey, and/or wafers. Tea plants are also for sale, in case you'd like to try your hand at creating your own tea from scratch.

THE COLLECTOR'S TEAPOT (MO)

❖ 800-724-3306

www.collectorsteapot.com

The Collector's Teapot designed their website as an offshoot of their ten-year-old mail-order catalog. On it, they feature a selection of best-selling and much-loved chubby Chatsford teapots from England, which they offer in two sizes—2-cup and 4-cup—in a variety of chipper hues, including blue, red, green, and yellow. The Chatsford is also available in restaurant-white, and in two florals—and there are matching mugs with integral infusers and lids. Other teapots to note are those by such respected firms as Spode, Wedgwood and Staffordshire. Teas, loose and bagged, are imported from Whittard, Yorkshire Gold, and Taylor's of Harrowgate. American teas made by The Republic of Tea are also on The Collector's Teapot list. In addition to the above, the company offers a number of tea-related books, specialty foods, and holiday items, as well as miniature tea sets.

CORTI BROTHERS (MO)

P.O. Box 191358
5810 Folsom Blvd,
Sacramento, CA 95819
❖ 916-736-3800

Darrell Corti imports estate-produced oolong and white (traditional, sun-dried) teas from Hong Kong tea merchant Wing-chi Ip, owner of the Lock Cha teashops. The "single-day harvest" teas are evaluated on site for their character to decide how long they should wither in the sun, be abraded in a rotating bamboo cylinder prior to fermentation, fired over charcoal, and rolled, kneaded and twisted by hand. Corti's teas originate at the Zhang family tea garden in China's Fujian province, and are processed there by the proprietors. Oolongs include Golden Cassia, Hairy Crab, and Tieguanyin; whites, Shoumei and Fuding Silver Needles. Corti sells these teas, through their newsletter, in two and four-tael (about 2.8 oz. and 5.6 oz.) quantities. Supplies are limited since, like wine, vintages sell out.

DAVID LEE HOFFMAN
SILK ROAD TEAS (MO)

P.O. Box 287, Lagunitas, CA 94938

❖ 415-488-9017

Hours: Telephone Monday through Friday

9 A.M. to 5 P.M., PST

David Lee Hoffman, a wholesale tea importer, owns a tea plantation in China, and has joint ventures with several established tea
gardens there. His selection of more than 100 mail-order teas
changes frequently, depending upon seasonal offerings; because of
this, customers know to telephone often for updated information
and catalogs. Green tea samplers are his specialty; all are hand-
picked from the first flush spring harvest and processed using
traditional skills.

FRANCHIA

www.franchia.com

The Koreans are justifiably proud of their wild green teas, which are grown on rocky slopes and harvested by hand, in part because green tea is integral to "Dah-do"–or Tea Tao–their revered Tea Ceremony, in part because the tea leaves are imbued with myriad health-enhancing qualities. HanGawi, a Korean restaurant in Manhattan (located at 12 E. 32 St.; 212-532-5788), recently decided to take their wild green tea public, so to speak, and offer it through their website, Franchia. Their Wild Green Tea is processed according to an exacting method entailing three separate roastings as well as a hand massage, and they sell three types: a Royal (or First Pick), a Second Pick, and a Third Pick. Dedicated, as they write, to "achieving balance and harmony in all things," they also offer their Wild Green Tea as part of a Starter Set consisting of a three-ounce box of tea, plus a bamboo tea scoop and a Personal Teacup (with lid, strainer, and coaster). Brewing instructions included with Franchia's informative brochure are precise and should be followed to the letter to achieve a quality sip with the appropriate "um and yang." Because of their strength, tea leaves can be brewed four additional times; steeping times vary with each brew.

As this edition was going into production, we noticed that Franchia is renovating a space on Park Avenue South near 32nd Street, for a Teahouse. If you are in the area, it should be open by the time you read this entry.

GRACE TEA COMPANY, LTD. (MO)

50 West 17th St., New York, NY 10011

❖ 212-255-2935

www.gracetea.com

Dick and Rita Sanders' personal and long-standing love affair with teas is manifest in their collection of 14 rare teas, all from Asia, which include their own, distinctive Connoisseur Master Blend and Owner's Blend, as well as their most popular Winey Keemun English Breakfast Tea. All Grace teas are hand-plucked and produced by traditional manufacture to produce loose tea of extraordinary quality—then hand-packed in black canisters in 1/2-lb. and 2-oz. (sampler) sizes. In Manhattan, Grace Rare Teas can be found at Zabar's, Dean & Deluca, and Grace's Marketplace, among other locations.

HARNEY & SONS (MO)

Tea Tasting Room/Shop: 11 Brook St., Salisbury, CT 06068
❖ 860-435-5051
Hours: Monday through Saturday 10 A.M. to 5 P.M.;
       Sunday 11 A.M. to 4 P.M.

Mail order: P. O. Box 665, Salisbury, CT 06068
❖ 888-427-6398
www.harney.com

The Harneys—father John and sons Mike and Paul—supply quality
tea to a number of New York City's hotels, museums, and department stores. The extensive gourmet section of their mail-order catalog and website offers a number of exotic teas that were not
available when we last went to press, notably four white teas and
a fifth composed of Pussimbing Silver Marbles which unfold while
brewing. A new line, monogrammed HT, is a selection of six original blends that reflect cross-cultural tastes; one of these is called
African Autumn, and mixes herbal rooibos with cranberry and
orange. These days, Harneys also carries tea blends specifically
formulated for iced teas. Some of these are infused with fruit flavors, such as mango/passion fruit; there's also an organic green.
Harneys makes up gift packages and samplers and they carry a
number of accessories as well as two books on tea: the *New Tea
Lover's Treasury* by James Norwood Pratt, and, by John Harney
with Joanna Pruess, a cookbook entitled *Eat Tea.*

HOLY MOUNTAIN TRADING CO.

www.holymtn.com

A visit to Holy Mountain's "site map" is an eye-opening experience. Besides the usual Welcome, Contact, and Catalog pages (of which there are many), the company offers discussions on tea processing, tea tasting, and etiquette, as well as information on jade, tea gardens and fountains—and legends of Buddha and other gods and goddesses. One extensive series of web pages explores the health benefits of various types of tea. The tea selection is wide ranging, with an emphasis on green teas from China, Japan, India and Vietnam. Jasmine teas, white teas, and pu-erh teas are also listed, as are black teas, both plain and scented. Pu-erh teas, including the earthy Camel Breath, come as "buttons," "mushrooms," bricks, cakes, or in 1/4-lb. or 1-lb. loose packs. Note: Holy Mountain's site also has a nationwide listing of dozens of venues where tea classes and tastings are held.

HONEST TEA

❖ 800-865-4736

www.honesttea.com

Stuck in NYC traffic on a recent rainy Saturday, we noticed the van in front of our city bus sported the above website address: honesttea.com. Logging onto the site, we were struck by the idealism of this young company (as we have been by a number of other sites selling tea and tea things). For one thing, the name Honest Tea refers to the fact that the owners barely sweeten their primary product, a bottled iced tea. The other is their dedication to the environment—all their teas are organic, and the tea bags for their whole-leaf teas are made with recycled materials. More importantly, Honest Tea is proud of its relationship with the Native American Crow Nation, with whom the company creates one of its most popular bottled (and bagged) teas: First Nation Organic Peppermint Herbal Tea. Other flavors include Moroccan Mint Green, Kashmiri Chai (in bags and bottles), Black Forest Berry, Decaf Ceylon, and Lori's Lemon Tea (in bottles only). Honest Teas can be ordered from a number of websites; log on to find out which they are.

IMPERIAL TEA COURT (MO)

1141 Powell St., San Francisco, CA 94133

❖ 800-567-5898

www.imperialtea.com

When Grace and Roy Fong opened the Imperial Tea Court in San Francisco's Chinatown a decade ago, it was heralded as the "first traditional Chinese teahouse in America." A former head of research and development for the International Tea Masters Association, Roy Fong knows his teas. The Fongs take especial pride in the top 100 prize-winning green teas of the China National Tea Rating Awards, which they offer for sale. The Imperial Tea Court's mail-order catalog and website change and update the selection of teas according to seasonal availabilities, but generally 60 to 100 (primarily) green teas are offered. Imperial Tea also invites you to join one of their Tea of the Month Clubs: the Four Seasons, the Six Month, or the full 12-month Year of Tea. Also offered are a variety of teapots and accessories, as well as an atmospheric CD to sip by: Cha Tao—The Way of Tea—with music played on traditional instruments.

IN PURSUIT OF TEA

❖ 866-TRUE-TEA

www.truetea.com

Friends and long-time travelers Alexander Scott and Sebastian Beckwith founded In Pursuit of Tea as the realization of a dream: "to bring the explorer's spirit to your day-to-day life." To that end, each spins his own travel tale on their mutual website, but, more significantly, the two offer hand-plucked, loose-leaf, organic "true teas" grown on small farms in remote parts of the world. Unadulterated by additives, the 30-plus teas in their inventory are sold in 1/4-lb. increments. As an introduction to the myriad styles of tea (including white and pu-erh), Scott and Beckwith present six teas in Asia-in-a-Box; an educational booklet accompanies the teas. While In Pursuit of Tea extols pure teas, they also sell herbal infusions and iced teas, as well as tea gear—including empty tea bags, so you can brew your own loose-leaf tea in the strength you prefer.

PURE SEASONS (MO)

❖ 800-721-3909

www.PureSeasons.com

Sausalito-based Pure Seasons is dedicated to presenting handcrafted items for the home that are made primarily from sustainable resources. They also believe that the taste of tea is influenced by the type of teapot in which you steep your tea leaves. They recommend a glass teapot for herbal brews, stoneware vessels for black teas, and light ceramics for green teas. A recent catalog featured two ceramics: one, a rotund, sand-colored teapot called the Nichibei, by artists Mikio Matsumoto and Cheryl Constantini, and the other, a ceramic teapot exhibiting a lustrous, deep-toned mottled patina—and, inside, an aquamarine glaze—by designer Helen Faibish. Pure Seasons also sells a number of green, black, and herbal teas, a tea tray, and organic honeys from Spain.

THE REPUBLIC OF TEA (MO)

8 Digital Dr., Suite 100, Novato, CA 94949

❖ 800-248-4832

www.republicoftea.com

As the mystical republic's first Minister of Leaves whimsically observed in an early newsletter: "Tea is contentment . . . Drinking tea, desires diminish and I come to see the ancient secret of happiness: wanting what I already have, inhabiting the life that is already mine." Well, you might want more than what you already have—in terms of tea, that is. These days, The Republic of Tea provides dozens of choices, many in their signature cylindrical boxes, as well as bottled iced teas and chais, tea-infused honeys and marmalades, and, new to the line-up, tea oil packed with Vitamin E and other natural antioxidants. According to The R of T literature, tea oil, used for cooking, contains less saturated fat than olive oil. Among their teas, The R of T offers 42 "kosher" blends. Gift items include a Black Tea Traveler's Silk Pouch with two mini-tins of tea, and the larger Have Tea Will Travel box, with 27.

SERENDIPITEA

❖ 888-TEA-LIFE

www.serendipitea.com

Like a number of other on-line purveyors of fine and exotic teas,
Serendipitea subscribes to an environmentally responsible philosophy, culling its leaves from tree estates where teas are grown
organically, and buds and leaves are plucked by hand. The range
of teas is wide. One of its more exotic chais is called Xocatlatl
Chai, which blends masala spice, vanilla, mint, chocolate and black
tea; the chai can be taken with or without milk. Another, Cha Cha
Chai, blends Assam tea with cinnamon, cloves, and cardamom.
Serendipiteas come in 4-oz. boxes. We noticed them at retail at
several shops around town, including Zabar's, and at Asia Society.

SIMPSON & VAIL, INC. (MO)

3 Quarry Rd., P.O. Box 765, Brookfield, CT 06804

❖ 800-282-8327

www.svtea.com

One of the oldest purveyors of tea in the United States, Simpson & Vail was founded in 1904 in Manhattan, and remained there until 1982 when the current owners, Jim and Joan Harron, moved the company to upstate New York. Today Simpson & Vail is located in Brookfield, CT; here the Harrons—including two of their children who have joined the business—maintain a retail store as well as a warehouse for mail orders. Simpson & Vail sells a wide selection of teas in every category. One of their more unusual offerings is a Chinese Tea Brick, a compressed Congou tea bearing an embossed design on top, which emulates a type once used as a form of currency. The inventory of tea things is equally vast, ranging from drip catchers and filters to cozies, caddies, and canisters.

STASH TEA (MO)

P. O. Box 910, Portland, OR 97207

Catalog requests: ❖ 800-800-TEAS or 503-684-9725

Orders: ❖ 800-826-4218 or 503-624-1911

www.stashtea.com

Also called A World of Tea, Stash Tea, founded in 1972, has received over 1.25 million hits since it launched its website back in July 1995. A veritable cornucopia of teas, tea foods and condiments, and tea things, Stash Tea also hosts a virtual tour of a tea estate in Darjeeling, India, offers over 100 recipes for dishes made with tea, and quotes a number of tea mavens. Needless to say, the site also offers lots of info regarding the history of tea and how tea is cultivated and harvested. It also supplies links to over 50 additional tea websites. And, it does all of this in over a dozen languages! As a final fillip, the site includes a bed and breakfast guide listing hundreds of B&Bs and inns around the country.

STRAND TEA COMPANY (MO)

P.O. Box 580, Sandy, OR 97055

❖ 888-718-6358

www.strandtea.com

Like many purveyors of tea, Jack and Judy Strand hew to the environmentally sound practice of purchasing only organic, estate-grown teas. Their website lists—and describes—over 100 fine teas of every category, including rooibos, honeybushes, and other herbal blends. The Strands also make up tea samplers, and they sell an assortment of tea things, too. If you are traveling to Oregon, check out Strand Tea's website for their schedule of tea tastings, which they offer in the Portland area.

TEA-CIRCLE

www.tea-circle.com

Long-time friends and devotees of the tea ceremony, Northern California–based Keiko Wright and Sachiko Chernin established this website to sell wares and utensils associated with this esteemed Japanese ritual. Their wares are presented as a simple alphabetized list; you click on the individual object to read and view the subset of items in that category. Tea Circle's inventory i exhaustive, and includes everything from tea powder strainers called *chafurui* to karamoji chopsticks to forks for sweets to okoï incense to tatami mats. The Tea Circle also presents a few select links; one of their favorites is to Minatoya, a Japanese sweets shop that now sells some of their *wagashi* through an English-lanï guage website.

TEARANCH/TEACUP

2207 Queen Anne Ave. N., Seattle, WA 98109

❖ 877-841-4890, call P.S.T.

www.tearanch.com

If you feel as if every workday were like a mountain to be climbed, you might be thrilled to find that you have the opportunity to sample an envigorating elixir known as Ed's Energy Tea. The tea was created by Seattle-based TeaRanch in honor of world-class mountaineer, Ed Viesturs, star of IMAX's *Everest* film. Ed's Energy Tea blends black and green teas with cinnamon, ginger, Siberian Ginseng, and other robust infusions and flavorings. TeaRanch sells over 120 other teas as well, in 1/4-, 1/2-, and full-lb. quantities. If you happen to visit Seattle, stop in at their retail shop, appropriately known as Teacup.

UPTON TEA IMPORTS (MO)

231 South St., Hopkinton, MA 01748

❖ 800-234-8327

www.uptontea.com

As a teenager, Tom Eck loved tea so much that he used to send to England for it. As an adult, he came to know a number of English—and French—tea tasters and prestige tea merchants. Today, a decade after founding Upton Tea Imports, Eck offers over 220 varieties of teas from China, Japan, India, Nepal, Sri Lanka, Taiwan, and Africa, which can be purchased by mail order or on-line. The user-friendly website catalogs teas by type; it also offers a range of teapots, accessories, such as caddies and infusers, and the Russell Hobbs electric kettle. Other helpful pages provide tips for storage, information on the caffeine content and health benefits of tea, and a primer on how much tea to order, including a tea conversion table. To round out its coverage, Upton Tea Imports reprints the lead articles from its quarterly newsletter; there's also an on-line tea dictionary explicating over 400 tea terms.

The Legendary Origins of Tea

Tea, it is said, was discovered in China in 2737 B.C., by Emperor Shen Nong. Attentive to matters of health and hygiene, the emperor was fastidious in such practices as boiling water. On one occasion, as he stoked the fire under his kettle, he plucked branches from a shrub close at hand and tossed them into the flames. A few leaves floated, by accident, into the water. As the leaves colored the water, the emperor, marveling at the fragrance that arose from the smoke, sipped the brew that resulted. Captivated by its flavor and by the stimulating feelings it generated, he hastened to advocate "ch'a," or tea, as an antidote for a plethora of ills from indigestion to lethargy.

Almost ten centuries later, poet Lu Yu wrote about the ceremony that had evolved around the preparation and presentation of tea. In his renowned *Book of Tea*, the poet described how the ritual mirrored an inward ethic which embraced respect and courtesy. Within this small, simple, generous—and beautiful—act, a harmony between host and guest could be realized, a harmony underlying all of life. Tea was a work of art.

Varieties of Tea

Tea connoisseurs cite over 3,000 varieties of tea, each with its own distinct character. As with fine wines, the quality of the tea is determined by climate, soil, and weather conditions, as well as on the expertise of the tea grower. Altitude also makes a difference; some of the most highly esteemed tea estates cling to the sides of mountains making access to the shrubs difficult and the plucking of the tea leaves (and buds) an arduous endeavor. Derring-do adds to a tea garden's mystique—and enhances the awe with which some rare premium teas are regarded.

Of all varieties of tea, almost 95 percent end up in tea bags. The rest comprise the prime-quality leaves and buds that are plucked—often by hand—for premium teas. Premium or not, what distinguishes any one tea from another is the process of its manufacture. This process is composed of several steps: plucking; withering the tea leaves to rid them of moisture; partially or fully drying and rolling them to release oils and enzymes (if desired); oxidizing (or fermenting) them, if desired; and, finally, drying them once again. Variations in the process result in leaves that can be distinguished by the depth and intensity of their color: black, green, oolong, and white. Tea may grow wild, but most are cultivated on tea plantations or on small estates known as tea gardens. Darjeelings are one family of Indian teas that often bear the name of the tea garden where they are produced. Darjeelings may be further defined by their harvest—or flush. The first flush occurs in the early spring and typically results in a delicate, refined tea; teas from the second (and later) flushes have more body.

The tea shrub may be allowed to mature organically, or it may be treated with pesticides. Finest premium teas are 100 percent organic. The leaves (and buds) of premium organic teas are plucked by hand at specific times of the year; every other stage of the process is also conducted by hand.

WHITES are the most delicate of teas. White tea leaves are harvested very early in the spring. Tightly furled, the balled-up leaves reveal a silvery cast. The leaves are withered for several hours, a process that causes them to lose almost half their original moisture-weight through evaporation. The leaves are then lightly roasted to remove all but ten percent of the remaining moisture—and to seal in their delicate flavor. Whites undergo no oxidation; they are not fermented.

GREEN teas are not oxidized either; after leaves and buds are plucked, they are usually spread out on trays made of bamboo and left to dry until most of the moisture has evaporated. The leaves are then swiftly heated to halt oxidation and prevent fermentation. Often the leaves are twisted or rolled to assume special shapes such as gunpowder pellets. As the tea steeps in the cup, the leaves gently unfurl.

OOLONG leaves are partially withered, shaken to release enzymes, then fermented as long as necessary to create a particular tea. Short fermentation results in a green tea-like tea; Pouchong is one example of such a tea. Longer fermentation imparts a more honey-like or amber tone to the tea.

BLACK teas undergo the lengthiest process. After plucking—by hand or machine—the tea leaves are withered, then rolled and re-rolled several times to release oils and enzymes. The leaves are fully oxidized, then fired. The firing halts oxidation at the precise moment required to lend character to a specific tea. These days, shredding the leaves with a machine (called a CTC because it Crushes, Tears, and Curls the leaves) during the withering process cuts fermentation time by half. CTC-assisted commercial grade teas generally have a uniform appearance and taste.

PU-ERH tea leaves are not oxidized, but they are fermented, and aged in caves for many years; the dampness in the caves lends them their distinctive earthy flavor.

FLAVORED teas receive their particular flavorings during the fermentation cycle; flavorings enhance a black- or green-based tea by imparting a particular "note" such as jasmine, ginger, or rose. Some of these teas mingle many different flavors.

A Short Glossary of Teas

The following are a few of the teas that are served loose and/or bagged at various New York venues. The ubiquitous Orange Pekoe is named for a grade of tea, not for a varietal.

Tisanes or infusions are herbals, not teas; note the glossary that follows.

TEA	COUNTRY OF ORIGIN	TYPE	TASTE
Assam	India	Black	Bright, hearty, malty, full-bodied, with a deep, almost mahogany hue
Ceylon	Sri Lanka	Black	Light, mellow, pungent, with a golden hue
Earl Grey, named for a British Prime Minister, Baron Charles Grey	China/India	Black	Citrusy, flavored with oil of bergamot
Darjeeling, "champagne of teas"; may be named for a specific tea garden	India,	Black	Light, delicate, flowery, with an amber hue
English Breakfast	India/Sri Lanka	Black	Robust, brisk, medium-bodied
Formosa Oolong	Taiwan	Oolong	Aromatic, flowery, light amber hue
Gemaichi	Japan	Green	Mixed with puffed rice
Gunpowder	China/Taiwan	Green	Slightly bitter, mildly astringent, yellow-green hue
Gyokuro	Japan	Green	Aromatic, herbaceous, jade hue
Irish Breakfast	China/Sri Lanka	Black	Stronger than English Breakfast, pungent, full-bodied
Jasmine	China	Green, with jasmine blossoms	Mild, delicate, fragrant, pale yellow-green hue
Keemun, "burgundy of teas"	China	Black	Sweet, flowery, full-bodied, with a deep amber hue
Lapsang Souchong	China	Black	Distinctive smoky flavor
Matcha	Japan	Green	Powdered Gyokuro, used in the Tea Ceremony
Pu-Erh	China	Black	Earthy, pungent, often molded into bricks, mushrooms and other shapes
Silver Needles	China	White	Delicate, mild, pale yellow hue

A Short Glossary of Herbal Teas

Herbal teas, also known as tisanes or infusions, are not really teas at all, but, because they are brewed in the same way as tea, they are thought to be in the same "family" of beverages. Composed of leaves and/or flowers, most tisanes are taken to aid digestion or to soothe the spirit; a number are believed to manifest other medicinal properties as well.

ROOIBOS, which are sometimes called RED TEAS (because of the reddish cast of their leaves), are herbals grown in South Africa. Rich in antioxidants and high in vitamin C, these herbal teas have long been appreciated for their perceived medicinal value. Because they contain very little tannin, prolonged steeping will not cause a rooibos to taste bitter; in fact, the tea benefits from an extended steeping time—up to 20 minutes or more. They can also be reheated. A relative of the rooibos is the honeybush, another caffeine-free herbal, with a citrusy accent, that also hails from South Africa.

TEA	ACTION
Chamomile	promotes relaxation
Ginger	relieves symptoms of a cold
Ginseng	boosts energy; counteracts infection
Lavender	relieves tension; prevents halitosis
Lemon Verbena	prevents indigestion; soothes nerves
Peppermint	promotes relaxation
Rosehip	boosts energy
Thyme	relieves headache
Verveine	aids and improves digestion

Storing Tea

When you purchase loose-leaf tea by the ounce, transfer it as soon as possible to an opaque container such as an airtight tin or a tea caddy and store it in a cupboard; your tea should stay fresh for months. Tea fades when exposed to light, so do not keep it in a glass container. Tea is adversely affected by moisture, so it should not be refrigerated or frozen. Tea bags should also be kept in a cool, dry location, away from light, so if you transfer them from the box in which they were purchased, make sure they are stored in a similar manner as loose-leaf tea.

The Health Benefits of Tea

Much has been written about how tea—especially green tea—will reduce blood pressure, help prevent liver and heart disease, lower cholesterol, improve digestion, and possibly avert stroke and a number of cancers, including cancer of the skin, colon, stomach, esophagus, breast, and prostate. In addition, because tea contains fluoride, it also fights the bacteria responsible for tooth decay and gingivitis. Some claim that tea also strengthens bones.

The reason tea is considered so healthy is because it contains polyphenols and flavenoids, which are naturally occurring compounds that act as anti-oxidants to ward off cancer-causing free radicals. Because white and green teas undergo virtually no processing (leaves are steamed, rolled, and dried, but not oxidized, which ferments the leaves), they contain the highest portion of these beneficial attributes.

Although tea enhances mental clarity, and, in the short term, is a stimulant, it typically does not cause either heightened nervousness or insomnia as coffee does, nor does it irritate the stomach. This is because the caffeine in tea is water soluble, which means that it passes through your digestive system more quickly than the non-water soluble caffeine contained in coffee.

Herbal teas are also regarded as healthful. Some of the most familiar and popular herbal teas (also called infusions or tisanes) are sipped to aid digestion and minimize bloating and flatulence; these include chamomile, peppermint, and verveine. Dieters may turn to chicory tea to curb their appetite and to berry teas to lower cholesterol. And insomniacs often find that lavender soothes them into slumber.

Despite their claims, some herbal teas may induce an allergic reaction. Nutritionists recommend that you try a new herbal tea in a very small dose—less than a quarter of a cup, at most—to make sure you do not have an adverse reaction to the flower, herb, or root that flavors that particular tea.

Even if you do not ingest tea for your health, you can still derive superficial health benefits from tea. Chilled, dampened tea bags, for example, are an antidote to sunburn, at once cooling the skin while tannins in the tea stanch the sting. Cool, moist tea bags may also reduce puffiness around the eyes—a good trick to try after a night on the town.

How to Make a Cup of Black Tea

1. Fill a kettle with cold water. (Cold water contains more oxygen than hot water; it is the oxygen that creates bubbles in the water to cause furled tea leaves to open and release their flavor.)

2. Bring water to the rolling boil for black tea. Do not overboil. (Overboiling causes the water to lose oxygen and can make the tea taste muddy.) Do not underboil. (Underboiling results in a thin tea that is both tasteless and tepid.)

3. While the water is coming to the boil, run hot water into the teapot. Swirl the water in the teapot, or let it sit for 2 minutes; pour out. The warmth of the pot will allow the dry tea leaves to begin to relax in anticipation of their immersion in the boiling water.

4. To the teapot, add one heaping teaspoon of loose tea for each cup. Do not use a teaball or infuser, if possible, as these confine the leaves.

5. Bring the teapot to the kettle, not vice versa. Every moment counts when preparing a cup of tea!

6. Pour the boiling water over tea leaves in the teapot. Let the tea steep for three to five minutes. Leaves will double in size as they steep. Brewing times vary, so consult your tea tin for recommended optimum time. (Overbrewing will cause the tea to stew and turn bitter.) Stir the tea gently after brewing.

7. Pour small amount of the tea through a strainer and into a cup. Dilute to taste with hot, boiled water. Add milk, if desired, or lemon. M.I.F.–Milk In First–was instigated to ensure that a fragile porcelain cup would not break when boiling water was poured into it. These days, you can add your milk before, or after, as you wish. Milk cuts the astringency of the tannin in tea. The addition of lemon originated in Russia. Take your pick. Or, drink tea neat as the purists do.

Black teas taste bitter after sitting in the pot too long, so they should be discarded after a single pour. (Oolong teas may be infused more than once; in fact, the Chinese believe that subsequent infusions–up to seven–bring increasing amounts of luck.)

After tea, the pot need only be rinsed. Soap or detergent can leave a residue that will affect subsequent pours. And then, feed your leaves to a compost pile, if you can.

How to Make a Cup of Green Tea

1. Bring warm water just barely to the boiling point; the water should be piping hot, but not actually bubbling. (Green tea leaves are very delicate and the action of the bursting bubbles of a rolling boil is too violent for them. Boiling water will also cause them to taste bitter.)

2. Rinse the pot with hot water, pour it off, then place a teaspoon or two of the leaves in the warmed pot.

3. Let water in the kettle sit for two to three minutes to cool slightly, then pour over the leaves.

4. Steep green tea leaves just a minute or so; strain and pour into cup.

5. Many green teas can be steeped at least three times before discarding the leaves.

Index by Neighborhood

CENTRAL VILLAGE/GRAMERCY PARK/MURRAY HILL

EAST MIDTOWN

About the Author

BO NILES is an editor and writer who specializes in design and decoration. She is a former Senior Editor at *Country Living* magazine and the author of a number of books including *White by Design, Living with Lace* and *Paperie: The Art of Writing and Wrapping With Paper.* Her collection of teaware includes her great-grandmother's silver tea service, four pink lusterware teacups, and a mug from the Pussy Willow Tea Room in Glasgow, Scotland.

About the Illustrator

SUSAN COLGAN is a painter whose still lifes are published in *Among Flowers,* a collaboration with poet Susan Kinsolving. She lives and works in New York and Berkshire County, Massachusetts.

Other City & Company Guides Available from Universe Publishing:

*City Baby: The Ultimate Guide for New York City Parents
from Pregnancy to Preschool*
Second Edition
By Pamela Weinberg and Kelly Ashton
$18.95
ISBN: 0-7893-0832-0

*Literary Landmarks of New York: The Book Lover's Guide to the Homes
and Haunts of World-Famous Writers*
By Bill Morgan
$16.95
ISBN: 0-7893-0854-1

New York's 50 Best Places to Take Children
Second Edition
By Allan Ishac
$12.95
ISBN: 0-7893-0836-3

New York's 50 Best Places to Find Peace and Quiet
Third Edition
By Allan Ishac
$12.95
ISBN: 0-7893-0834-7

*City Wedding: A Guide to the Best Bridal Resources in New York, Long
Island, Westchester, New Jersey, and Connecticut*
Second Edition
By Joan Hamburg
$18.95
ISBN: 0-789-308-568

The Cool Parents' Guide to All of New York:
Excursions and Activities In and around Our City that Your Children Will
Love and You Won't Think Are Too Bad Either
Third Edition
By Alfred Gingold and Helen Rogan
$14.95
ISBN: 0-789-308-576

New York's 100 Best Little Hotels
Third Edition
By Allen Sperry
$14.95
ISBN: 0-789-308-592

Heavenly Weekends
Second Edition
By Susan Clemett and Gena Vandestienne
$14.95
ISBN: 0-789-308-584

And Coming Soon:

New York's 50 Best Places to Enjoy Dessert
By Andrea DiNoto and Paul Stiga
$14.95
ISBN: 0-789-309-998

The New York Book of Wine
By Matthew DeBord
$14.95
0-789-309-971

New York's 50 Best Places to Renew Body, Mind, and Spirit
By Beth Donnelly Cabán and Andrea Martin, with Allan Ishac
$14.95
0-789-308-355